Seductive
Delusions

Seductive
Delusions

Exposing Lies about Sex

Gerard Henry

MOODY PUBLISHERS

CHICAGO

Edited by Kathryn Hall
Interior design: Ragont Design
Cover design: Marc Robinson, Vision Rocket Design
Cover image: IStockPhoto (Istockphoto.com)
Photographer: Gerenme

Library of Congress Cataloging-in-Publication Data

Henry, Gerard W.
  Seductive delusions : exposing lies about sex / Gerard Henry.
    p. cm.
  Includes bibliographical references.
  ISBN 978-0-8024-5716-5
  1. Chastity. 2. Sex—Religious aspects—Christianity. I. Title.

BV4647.C5H46 2010
241'.66—dc22

                                                    2010006959

1 3 5 7 9 10 8 6 4 2

Printed in the United States of America.

This book is dedicated to my fellow sisters and brothers who are committed to overcome every delusion faced with and purposes in their heart to perpetuate a godly legacy for their family and friends.

Contents

Foreword

I will never forget my first meeting with Gerard Henry. It was hard to believe that he was only eighteen years old. I was impressed with the clarity of his personal vision and his passion to reach his generation with the gospel. When I say generation, I mean his entire age group and beyond. What a vision for a teenager! I realized that his boldness was born out of faith and conviction.

At that time it was easy for me to commit to mentoring such a promising young man. In the early years he talked about the need to speak to the leading music and film stars of the day. He wanted to have input into their message and their personal lives. To many, these desires may have seemed like a pipe dream. Today it is obvious that his words were prophetic. Every time I saw a promo for his program on BET, I thought to myself, *He's walking in his destiny!*

Gerard is a gifted communicator with a unique ability to connect with his culture. Like Sean "P. Diddy" Combs, Spike Lee, or Kirk Franklin, he has an ability to speak to the complexities of today's youth scene. What sets Gerard apart from many motivational conference speakers is his ability to communicate a positive message on sensitive matters in an electrifying and galvanizing way. The essence of his unique speaking gift is captured in his work. Gerard's message is not religious, stilted, or guilt producing.

The pages you are about to read will help people of all age groups come to grips with one of the most important topics of this millennium—sexuality and the new sexual ethic. As Gerard tells his own story and values, he conveys vision, encouragement, and hope to his readers.

I predict that this fast-paced, easy-to-read work will become a quotable reference and a most popular gift.

—Bishop Harry R. Jackson Jr., Master of Divinity
Pastor, Hope Christian Church, Beltsville, Maryland

Preface

Sex is everywhere these days. Turn on the TV, glance up at a billboard, or walk through the mall, and chances are you'll be bombarded with sexual images. It's quite a contrast from even fifty years ago. But what message is this increasing openness sending? What's behind that model's seductive smile or sultry stare? It is now widely accepted that we can openly talk about sex at almost any given time. But as a result, are we as a society more sexually fulfilled?

Don't misunderstand me. I'm not advocating a return to the age when sexual issues were never discussed in polite company, let alone public forums. Such "prudish" attitudes toward sex are actually based on the gross misconception that physical intimacy is something shameful. This belief has caused many parents to be afraid to communicate with their children about the sensitive subject of sex—a subject on which children desperately need guidance. Parents must teach their children about the true reason why sex was created by God. As well, it's just as important for them to discuss age-appropriate behaviors toward sex and the many dangers that lie in wait when bad choices are made—"putting the cart before the horse" with regard to choosing to become sexually active. Such negligence has forced each generation of budding adolescents to discover the answers for themselves, which has contributed to the seductive delusions that people have experienced—and in many cases the results have been tragic.

However, I do challenge our present-day culture's rather casual handling of the subject of sex, when, in fact, sex is a significant part of our human identity. I believe this of human sexuality has caused too many of us to embrace a delusion and settle for less than the best in our own sex lives. It is almost impossible to talk about true sexual fulfillment without at least addressing the messages put forth in advertising, music, television, movies, and so on. In this new era of openness, not only do we have the input of our family, peers, and religion of choice to shape our views about this powerful subject, but a constant barrage of media-generated images as well.

Having been a member of the media myself, I am well acquainted with the use of these images. As a young man, my own ideas toward sex-related issues have developed a great deal over time. In this process of personal growth, I have become more than a little concerned about the myth that our culture perpetuates, which I have found to be full of empty promises. That is why I wrote this book: to share my own discoveries about obtaining true sexual fulfillment and to provide information that I am thankful to now know.

Before we go any further into this "controversial topic" (as some might call it), let me also clarify what I am not trying to do. I am not presenting myself as a "sexpert," seeking to provide explicit hints to help your wildest fantasies come true. I am also not looking for an opportunity to merely express my personal opinion. What I am addressing is the side of sex that doesn't come out in the soap operas, music videos, and sultry movies—the side that makes us vulnerable—and sometimes wounded.

To understand my point, I'll need you to ask yourself this question: "Who am I?" Now, let me be more specific: Are you strictly a biological creature whose sexual desires are nothing more than raging hormones that motivate the procreation of your species? Or are you more than that? If you honestly believe that your sexuality is no deeper than animal instinct, then put this book back on the shelf. However, if you recognize that your sexual desire indicates something beyond your basic impulses, then I think you will find the information presented here insightful.

I suggest that you are a spiritual being and that

there is some aspect of your identity that transcends mere biology and raw emotion. This spiritual being I speak of is how God made you. Our spirits are connected to Him, which also allows us to communicate with Him on an intimate level. If you can accept this, then it shouldn't be too much of a stretch to accept that sex is more than just a physical experience—it is a spiritual one. My premise is that sex is a spiritual as well as an emotional and physical act. Because of this, it cannot be experienced at its best unless all three aspects of our identity (spiritual, emotional, physical) are involved in a healthy way.

What do you think of our culture and what it's done to our sexuality? Do you believe that we have exploited this precious God-given gift and turned it into something ugly and reprehensible outside of the context in which it was given? I believe that our culture's corruption of human sexuality has promoted delusions about sex that are not only untrue, but also destructive to individuals and society as a whole. My hope is that this book will help the process of destroying these harmful delusions and direct the hearts and minds of readers toward healthy and fulfilling relationships.

Introduction
The Playas' Club

LOOKIN' FOR SOME LOVIN'

It was in the late spring following my sophomore year of high school. I was definitely planning to get into something—ready for an exciting summer filled with lust and adventure. The previous summer saw me lose my virginity to a girl who had moved back to my area from the West Coast. She had made it clear that she wanted to hook up again this particular summer. Even though I suspected that she wanted more of a commitment, I knew I could just "play the role" of the devoted boyfriend.

As far as I was concerned, life was all good. I was eyeing another female who was ready and willing to "mess around" over summer break. The girl was fly and the good news was that nobody in my circle at school really knew her. That made it virtually a risk-free proposition. We just had to schedule our period of "flings" and move on.

I was living the dream of most of my boys— and lovin' it.

Opportunities didn't even stop there. My third "project" was a Christian girl from a private school who lived nearby. She wasn't allowed to receive phone calls from boys, so she would call me—a lot! Well, my girl told me that she dreamed about the two of us getting married, having babies, making our home together—you know the script. This was crazy stuff as far as I was concerned, but I knew that if I played to her fantasies, it would be enough to persuade her to give me her virginity. So far, our relationship had consisted of meeting at the library. But we had agreed that this summer we'd take our friendship a step further. Translation for me: It was on! Is that the mark of a true *playa* or what?

I was definitely with all of that. I felt like it couldn't get much better than this. I was living the dream of most of my boys—and lovin' it. The fact is that we were all strongly influenced by the flow of society at that time. It was one where the social norm painted a picture identifying the guy with the most girls—or at least, the most options—as being a *playa*.

Fast forward to today and the *playa* thing is off the charts. But, at that time, if I had to play the role—that was all right with me. My hormones were raging just like everybody else's. At least, that's how I saw it. Besides, I had a two-fold objective. To me, hookin' up with the "honeys" was the natural way to not only gratify my urges, but to also establish my manhood. And that was all good.

I had it all figured out. I was smart enough to know my limitations and how to work around them. I knew my physical appearance was only average, but I knew that girls would fall just as quickly for charm, personality, and the prospect of security in a relationship.

PLAYIN' THE GAME

I remember when I lost my virginity. The girl I was with asked me if I "loved" her. For me, there was no relationship between us—just sex. We were just chillin' with each other. She had been cool with one of my ex-girlfriends from junior high school. I'm to admit that I don't even remember how we hooked up in the first place.

Still, when she dropped that heavy question, despite how much I wanted to have sex, I didn't want to lie. Instead of answering her straight up, I looked at her and asked, "What do you think?" Just the implication that I loved her was enough for her to yield her body. That's when I learned firsthand how so many females are willing to give sex for the promise of what they think is love. I also learned that "a nice guy" like me could manipulate and deceive just about anyone to get sex.

KEEPIN' IT REAL

In many ways, I was a typical teenager. My need to be liked made me want people to give me respect. Whether it was through my performances on stage, playing football, or being with the ladies—I needed others to approve of me. As a result, I placed a lot of value on how girls saw me. I felt good about the fact that I had managed to steer clear of drugs and alcohol. These were temptations that continued to entrap many of my peers. Yet girls remained my weakness (or, as I saw it, my strength). I was sure that having the opportunity to juggle three different ladies, who were all fine enough to score in any man's book, would help me prove myself in everyone's eyes—including my own.

However, I'm happy to say that God had other plans for me that summer. I don't know if you believe in God or how you feel about Him. But that summer, I met the Creator of the universe. He radically changed the course of my life. You see, I grew up in a traditional Christian home in Teaneck, New Jersey. I believed in the Bible. I had even invited Jesus into my heart for three straight nights when I was twelve years old, because I thought that's what you were supposed to do. However, after I was baptized, as one was expected to do, I should have been on my way. I thought I had made all of the right moves. But still, it wasn't enough to keep me from the temptations associated with a boy going through puberty.

I felt good about the fact that I had managed to steer clear of drugs and alcohol. Yet girls remained my weakness.

Suddenly, that all changed. The events of the summer before I entered my junior year blew me away. Somehow it all made sense out of what had happened to me when I was twelve. There is no doubt in my mind that when I accepted Jesus into my life, it showed me my spirituality and in my heart I knew I was in a deeper place of understanding who God really is. This all went down while I was attending a home Bible study with some college students from

Rutgers University. (One of the students happened to be an older sister of a friend of mine.)

Anyway, as we prayed during the close of the study, I became acutely aware of God's presence. I cannot fully articulate the feeling that came over me but, right at that moment, every ounce of hunger and thirst that was in my heart became totally satisfied. Instead of just inviting God into my heart, I began finding my identity in Him.

I felt a sense of completeness and security that I had never experienced before. And it was far beyond the temporary satisfaction I was looking for with those three girls. I realized that Jesus was not only my Savior, but He had also become my Friend. This friendship could not be compared to anything else in this world—not even what I felt was the pleasure I enjoyed by having sex.

THE AWAKENING

It just so happened that the Christian girl soon stopped calling. When she faded from my life it caused me to wonder if her mother's prayers and parental authority had intervened. In some way, it seemed like more than a coincidence that her calls stopped around the same time a change had taken place in me.

In the same way, the girl from my school who was open to anything that I wanted to explore also stopped calling. Actually, my boy saw some potential in her and they hooked up. As it turned out, that was a "snooze-lose" situation for me. It took too long for me to make a move on the "opportunity," so he seized the moment. I was partially hurt over it, but I wasn't serious about her, so I didn't let it get to me. I knew that I wasn't going to hold up "my end of the bargain" anyway.

The girl from the West Coast was the most difficult to cut loose because she wanted to pick up where we left off the previous summer. It didn't take her long to see that I was serious about my newfound commitment to God—which included no sex. Since she made it clear to me that she didn't share similar feelings, we parted ways.

At last, the reality of salvation had touched my heart. As the Word puts it:

> *"If anyone is in Christ, he is a new creature; the old things passed away; . . . new things have come"* (2 Corinthians 5:17).

In essence, my life changed on a dime once I seriously committed myself to Christ! All along, I had been driven by my animalistic nature. Now it was clear, the reason why casual sex left me feeling so empty was all of a sudden a "no-brainer." Even the physical satisfaction which, let's face it, is pretty automatic for guys, quickly dissipated.

My spiritual eyes and ears were opened, and I recognized that I was a new person on the inside. It felt good to know that I didn't have to let my old character control me any longer. I became aware that I couldn't engage in the physical act of sex without giving away part of myself—spiritually and emotionally. It was now apparent that looking for physical pleasure or ego gratification left me longing for something more.

I'M KEEPIN' IT TO MYSELF

No doubt about it. I learned a great lesson: My self-worth did not depend on what others thought of me. This knowledge made me want to make the most of my life. To make it happen, I was confronted with the fact that I needed to keep myself sexually pure. As a result, my entire outlook on sex took a drastic turn. Sex became sacred to me. It was not something I would engage in, talk about, or think about having with just anyone. I was determined to reserve my body for just one person—my wife. And because I hadn't met her yet, I knew that I had some waiting to do.

Through this change of heart I found that it takes more strength and courage to save sex for marriage than it does to yield to the temptations of our carnal instincts.

Making the appropriate changes in my behavior required that I guard my thoughts and not allow my eyes to disrobe a woman. It required me to not feed my eyes and ears with information that would arouse me sexually. It required me to avoid situations that were conducive to sexual intimacy. Yes, I know that this is a very difficult thing to do. But, if you're serious about God and the change He has made in your life, then it's time to show the world that part of being a man of God is doing away with sexual immorality. That part of being a man is to show some self-control by making a conscious decision to serve and please Him and not yourself.

Making the appropriate changes in my behavior required that I guard my thoughts and not allow my eyes to disrobe a woman.

All in all, I had to allow myself to become vulnerable to criticism from those who still viewed sexual behavior in the same way that I once did. This required a willingness to be misunderstood—especially by young people like myself, who still didn't "get it." If I appeared to be weak for the sake of remaining abstinent—then bring it on. I was now determined and committed to being sexually pure until the day I got married. That was huge for me, but I was ready to take on the challenge.

Ultimately, I was blessed to discover that being a part of the *playas'* club is not the place to be. The driving force behind my youthful escapades was nothing more than seductive delusions, which I now realize were keeping me from understanding what sex at its best is all about. Make sure to take the opportunities that come when you hear that still small voice in your head telling you that engaging in sexual immorality is wrong. Make sure that you really listen and seek God's face to help you turn your life around and live it solely for Him. It's a day-to-day, moment-by-moment choice we have to make to keep choosing the things of God. I promise that you will feel so much better about yourself as you continue to choose God.

After reading this book, my hope is that you too will discover the blessing of true sexual fulfillment. Just as it was for me, your discovery will more than likely require you to make some changes to your current thinking and behavior. In the end, taking the time and effort to learn the useful information contained in this book will help you decide not to settle for the societal myths that are generally touted about sex. At that moment in time, your entire being will be prepared for a sex life that not only you and your marriage partner will be grateful for—but also one with which God will be pleased.

Love
or Lust?

Although that summer I had made a decision to save sex for marriage, I still had to deal with the sexual passions stirring within me. Prior to my encounter with God, I was extremely lustful. Whether it was messin' around with girls in the back stairways of our high school, in the woods, or at their crib—it didn't matter. Hey, the game was about self-gratification. In fact, some of the things that attracted me to the entertainment industry were that it offered money, fame, and plenty of "honeys"—all of which were extremely important to me at the time.

However, dealing with that attitude had become a major battle for me, once the God factor kicked in, because those desires did not instantly disappear. Instead, I had an internal war going on as I tried to cope with a set of emotions that were contrary to the nature of God. "*God is love*" (1 John 4:16). Once I had been confronted with His love and allowed that to be the driving force with which I saw everything around me, it was more difficult for me to yield to lust.

I can remember the first party I went to after encountering God's love. I was enjoying the music and the food and having a great time. It was all good until I made my way to the dance floor and got close to a young lady. I will never forget how awkward I felt dancing so close and rubbing against her body. It really felt unnatural, and to my surprise, that shocked me. As I was working through this inner conflict, the Lord helped me understand that I felt awkward because His holy presence doesn't include "freak dancing." Behavior and movements that were formerly driven by lust didn't bring the same satisfaction once I was driven by God's love within me. I can also recall opportunities in college to have relationships with sisters that would involve sexual intimacy. In each case, I explained how I could not offer them myself because I was aware of a greater love than that which they were searching for. Although they weren't aware of it, they were attracted to me because of God's love and presence in my life rather than any physical attribute that I had to offer. It was and still is my passionate awareness of God's love and presence in my life that keeps me from engaging in anything that would cause distance in my relationship with God.

Too many of us have settled for a counterfeit motivation in our sex lives: lust.

Love is one of the most powerful motivating forces for human behavior. Most major religions teach and most people believe that love is virtuous and is something all human beings desire. I contend that giving and receiving unconditional love are one of the most basic human needs that stems from our emotional and spiritual nature. Can you imagine being with someone who loves you just because you are who you are? In other words, they admire, respect, accept, and adore you. There is no pressure to perform or live up to a certain standard by which you will receive their love—it's unconditional. Even when they find out the bad and the ugly sides of who you are, their love is still present and strong. They just want to be with you because you're—you. This exchange of perfect love is found in intimacy, and it is this intimacy that our hearts and spirits need, to experience a deeper level of meaning when it comes to sex. However, too many of us have settled for a counterfeit motivation in our sex lives: lust.

Movies and television shows that glamorize

uncommitted sex create a false impression in the minds of viewers. Such entertainment choices suggest that unbridled lust offers the most appealing and fulfilling sexual experience. They also frequently espouse the idea that there are many "shades of gray" between love and lust, boldly endorsing the concept of situational ethics over unchanging convictions.

That one-night stand in the movie *Titanic* or that extramarital affair in any given soap opera are portrayed as expressions of love between two people who should otherwise be in a lasting relationship. If it were not for their individual circumstances, which are "tragically" keeping them apart, the two lovers would gladly exchange their unhappy lives to be together forever. Right. In real life these circumstances translate into confusion as the people involved typically try to justify their actions.

Sadly, the young lady to whom I lost my virginity could have easily been influenced by the impetus of this kind of dramatic and impressionable, but misguiding portrayal. She could believe that I "loved" her simply because she didn't really know how to distinguish real love from the lust that was actually motivating me. I must reiterate that, along with her, I was also a victim to the persuasiveness of media influence and societal pressure. Believe in yourself, not in the lust of your flesh. You are worth so much more than that. Ask God about it; He'll tell you and show you that much and more.

WHAT IS LOVE?

The fundamental difference between love and lust is that lust is self-centered, whereas love is other-centered. I want to share my thoughts on a familiar passage of the Bible that appears every year on Valentine's Day cards across the country. It is taken from 1 Corinthians 13:4 and reads: *"Love is patient, love is kind and is not jealous; love does not brag and is not arrogant."*

> # The fundamental difference between love and lust is that lust is self-centered, whereas love is other-centered.

Love is patient. Lust is impatient. Love has no problem waiting for sex because it is patient. A man who tells his girlfriend that he just can't wait to have sex, because he loves her so much, is lying. He can wait; he just doesn't want to place the well-being or wishes of his girlfriend above the gratification of his own cravings. Even if the sex is completely consensual, you have to ask questions such as these: Are

31

those who jump hastily into bed really loving each other, or did their basic urges just happen to coincide? Would a friend take advantage of another friend's vulnerability? Can I trust what just happened to mean that we will be committed to each other for the rest of our lives? Will he or she respect me after this if I tell him or her I don't want to be intimate with him or her anymore?

Love is kind. Lust is unkind. Love considers the needs and desires of the other person first. It will go to any lengths to avoid unnecessarily hurting its partner. Lust will weigh its options and see what works in its own interest. It may appear to act kindly, but only to gain something in return. This unkindness and selfishness saturates the mindset of the individual motivated by lust. Do you want to be involved in a relationship where you are always wondering if he or she really loves you?

Many women are aware of the lustful intentions of a charming man who has a hidden agenda. Unfortunately, these same women will often go out with the guy anyway, allowing him to treat them as objects instead of giving them the respect that a woman truly deserves. How sad. By the same token, many women will use their sexuality to manipulate men, knowing that most men will do just about anything for sex. Flirtatious glances and suggestive words will easily have a lot of men buying them gifts or taking them to dinner in a heartbeat. This is also a demonstration of the unkindness that is characteristic of lust. The bottom line is, "I will use you to get what I want." Is it really worth giving up your peace of mind, allowing her to manipulate you into getting her own way?

Love is kind. Lust is unkind.

Another trait of love is trustworthiness. Love doesn't envy; it isn't jealous of other friends or other things that attract the mate's attention. Love isn't threatened by anything in the loved one's past. On the other hand, lust, by its very nature, is extremely demanding. It will take and take and take until there is nothing left to be taken.

Love doesn't brag—not only about sexual exploits —but about itself in general. Think about the words used to refer to sex in settings such as locker rooms, barber shops, beauty salons, nightclubs, sporting events, sleepovers, and so on. We've all heard them. Ask yourself, do any of these phrases suggest love, intimacy, or caring for another person?

Remember, love's main concern is the wellbeing of the one who is the object of its love. The main concern of lust is the gratification of the one who is in lust. When applied to intercourse itself, it only makes sense that the couple who is focused on giving and pleasing each other will be more satisfied in the end, as opposed to the couple where one or both members only want to gratify themselves. There are many sexually frustrated men and women as a result of lust-based relationships. By the way, that incredible, simultaneous orgasm between two strangers passing in the night—happens far more often onscreen than off.

CAN LUST BE POSITIVE?

Having just referred to the Bible for a working description of love, I want to acknowledge that there are a large number of people out there who don't buy into the idea that lust is a negative thing. They don't consider lust as being a sin against God. Some see the plea-sure gained from sex to be a legitimate end in itself; therefore any sex, if it is pleasurable, is good sex. I beg to differ.

Teenagers are particularly vulnerable to lust because of the aforementioned characteristics of impatience, pride, bragging, and so on. These traits are generally behaviors associated with emotional immaturity. Without understanding the important differences between love and simple desire, such immature behavior, coupled with physically maturing bodies, can be a recipe for disaster. When teenagers engage in premarital sex, their emotional growth can be severely damaged. Having established a behavioral pattern of shallow sex early in life, they often become adults who behave like shallow juveniles when it comes to intimate relationships.

Unfortunately, sexually active youth feel that they have discovered all there is to know about physical intimacy. As a result, they have inadvertently accepted that lust is as good as it gets. While few people will admit that one of their primary goals in life is the pursuit of meaningless pleasure, we are encouraged to find pleasurable escapes from the pressures of our contemporary existence.

Recall my previous example of entertainment media. Specifically, I am referring here to the kind of movie or program that associates a brief affair between two consenting adults, who happen to be "getting over" other relationships, with the need to get drunk or smoke a joint once in a while. This activity appears to be perfectly harmless for the characters involved, and no one gets hurt. Yet, it is extremely damaging for the young, impressionable minds of youth, who are open to any idea that would make them appear more "in the game." This is simply because they don't know any better and are trying to find their way through and make a place for themselves in this life.

As an aspiring actor/producer/director, I am not against the media dealing with reality, no matter how ugly it may sometimes be. What concerns me is that they are sending a misguided message and the real consequences of the behaviors portrayed are seldom shown. That fact leaves a sizeable portion of the population at a great disadvantage.

For instance, we see many movies celebrating teenagers as they discover their sexuality and develop interpersonal relationships. But we don't hear nearly enough about the teenage couple whose aspirations to attend college are thwarted by an unplanned pregnancy. I know of one such couple who began dating at age sixteen. The girl had a desire to become a doctor, and the guy wanted to become a chemical engineer. They shared their dreams of the colleges they wanted to attend. They even talked about their future and where they would live after receiving their respective degrees.

Unfortunately, as the relationship progressed, they decided to become sexually active, which led to the girl becoming pregnant. Although they both managed to graduate from high school, their college aspirations were never fulfilled. The boy went on to attend a local university and took a menial job in an effort to support the baby. Because of his work hours, he was often too tired to study and his grades suffered.

Furthermore, due to complications with the pregnancy, the girl's plans to begin college were delayed until the spring semester. After the baby was born, she was often late to class because she had to not only get herself ready in the morning but also take care of the baby's needs. There were other times when she couldn't get a babysitter and that prevented her from going to class at all.

Several years later, the young couple is still together. She is working as a cashier at a discount retail store, and he works at an auto parts store. This is a far cry from becoming the doctor and engineer they had hoped to be. It is regrettable that this story is true and there are so many others with similar details.

Whether it is the trauma of having an abortion, contracting a sexually transmitted disease, or the emotional damage incurred from sharing intimacy with a person whom you are not committed to for life, the consequences of premarital sex last long after the brief act of pleasure. With the rising epidemic of teen pregnancies and sexually transmitted diseases (STDs), we have to find a way to assist teenagers in their growing years. In most cases they are raising themselves, thereby making their own decisions to have sex—and in most cases they have their lives take a major turn from the direction it was supposed to go. Let's get involved. Become a volunteer at your local Boys and Girls Club of America or local church youth group, or some other church or school. It's time we make a difference in their lives so they can see that they do have a future.

Moreover, the irony that is rarely addressed in the media is that lust inevitably leads to loneliness and frustration. Acts of lust may temporarily soothe the

Seductive Delusions

pain or hurt that an individual is experiencing, but the ultimate result will be more pain. Why is this? Why is lust unable to meet our deepest needs? It is because we are more than just physical beings. We long for intimacy on a deeper level than the mere physical. If lust is our motivation and lust focuses on self, how can we ever be intimate with someone else? The bottom line is, we cannot focus on self alone without feeling the pain and suffering that is caused by emptiness and the lack of true companionship.

> **The consequences of premarital sex last long after the brief act of pleasure.**

WHAT IF WE REALLY LOVE EACH OTHER?

My argument is that lust is the motivation for having sex with someone to whom you are not married. We'll get into why this is the case in the next two chapters. For now, consider this simple fact: In any relationship, there are only two possible outcomes. You will either stay together forever in marriage, or you will break up at some point.

When I talk about sex at its best, I am referring to a deep intimacy that comes from the innermost part of your being. This type of intimacy is very often taken too lightly—even though it requires a level of vulnerability that you should not dare have with anyone who is not committed to you for life. To do so is to bring about sometimes very harsh consequences, and frankly it's rather delusional. Think about it—you are revealing your complete nakedness with another individual. In that moment, the way in which you look, smell, and express yourself both verbally and nonverbally is revealed. That is a tremendously personal, extremely intimate, and most sacred disclosure.

I can still recall how I became disgusted with the females with whom I shared intimacy. I lost respect for them because I had fulfilled my conquest. The thrill of the hunt was completed, and I did not want the responsibility of a committed relationship. I wanted the benefits without the responsibility or commitment. This is the mentality of many men today, both young and old. And now, sadly, many of our women have adopted the same attitude to protect themselves from getting hurt. And it doesn't work. Looking for love in all the wrong places will most assuredly have you walking away empty-handed. Everybody loses. Nobody wins. How sad.

Lack of commitment means lack of love. Even if you are already engaged, true love is patient, as we mentioned before. A person who genuinely loves you will be happy to wait until after your wedding ceremony. Too many couples get "engaged" without a ring or even a wedding date in order to convince themselves (and others) that they are truly committed to each other.

> When I talk about sex at its best, I am referring to a deep intimacy that comes from the innermost part of your being.

In reality, if you aren't married, you will always be guessing about your partner's love for you. How risky. Most people's emotional issues regarding rejection and abandonment can be traced to a parent or another close individual who failed in the area of commitment. If this describes you, please understand that unconditional love (this is in regard to any relationship) is dedicating oneself to someone else for a lifetime. Even though it may seem scary, it is possible to achieve this status with God's help. Sometimes this requires a leap of faith. But if you believe that God was with you when you decided to allow this person into your heart, He will also remain with you after you have invited him or her to share your truest feelings.

When I made the decision to propose to my wife, I worked through much internal conflict and wondered whether she would respond favorably. She had stated that she valued our friendship and was open regarding marriage, but she wasn't sure. I knew that if I communicated with certainty and gave her a diamond ring, my actions would show her that I was serious about committing the rest of my life to her and thereby persuading her to respond.

I took the leap of faith based on my knowledge and the fact that what I felt in my heart toward her, I did not feel toward any other woman. It was something that wasn't driven by her physical beauty, her sweet voice, her love for God, or anything that she could do for me—all of which attract me to her. The love I felt for Terry was just because . . . I felt that there was nothing she could do to cause me to stop loving her. I knew it was unconditional. I knew it was love.

To conclude this discussion of love and lust, consider this illustration. A starving man eats out of a garbage can because he is hungry. He is aware of the fact that the container is filled with rotten food and disease. Despite the fact that rats and flies eat there too, out of necessity, he will search through the debris because it is the only thing close to food that he can find.

When people are driven by necessity, they will eat garbage in the absence of healthy food. In a similar way, some people will settle for lust in the absence of real love because they are doing so out of a deep need. Just like garbage, when people partake of lust, it brings a lot of unwanted danger and disease along with it.

But here's the difference. Lust has a dangerous tendency to cloud our ability to make good decisions. In this case, the reality is that we have a clear choice and the consequences of lust far outweigh any short-term pleasure gained.

Too many couples get "engaged" without a ring or even a wedding date in order to convince themselves (and others) that they are truly committed to each other.

2

Making a Love Connection

Go into a club on a Friday night in any city in America, and the scene is the same. You will find women wearing heavy makeup, jewelry, and outfits that make one wonder if they're really strippers out on the town—on their "night off." You will also observe lots of hungry men who are scoping out the landscape, looking for a good time. Sure, some people are there just to dance, drink, and forget the cares of the week, but most are trying to "meet somebody." Then again, some are really hoping that they'll make a true "love connection." At 1 a.m. in a crowded, smoky room filled with strangers, no less. Many others would be happy with a hookup that might even last through the weekend.

Socially acceptable dating used to mean that a young man would visit a young lady's home to court her, always under the watchful eye of her father. Eventually, if everything worked out, he would ask the protective dad for the young lady's hand in marriage. However, things have changed drastically. The singles scene today is not for the faint of heart. Amid all the flirting and pickup games lurk disease and serious emotional problems that claim more victims every day. Bodies are ruined by STDs. Self-esteem is destroyed. Marriages are ruined before they've even had a fair chance at success.

For all of these reasons and more, I think it's time that we take a look at why the virtually archaic picture of the dating scene wasn't so bad after all.

YOU'RE ONLY YOUNG ONCE

Our culture seems to relish youth as a time when we must try everything at least once. Premarital sex is often viewed as part of the normal singles' experience. There are plenty of people who are sexually active who have no intention of marrying anytime in the near future because of age, career goals, or a variety of other reasons. Some are involved in a "monogamous" relationship, that is, having a boyfriend or girlfriend whom they sleep with without entertaining serious thoughts of marriage. However, many are content to go from bed to bed pretty casually, making promiscuity their lifestyle.

I know that I was headed down this path, this vicious cycle, this destructive pattern of promiscuity. Even so, I had actually made a decision, after inviting Jesus into my heart at age twelve, to not have sex until marriage. I can remember publicly taking a stance in my middle-school locker room and being teased because I was missing out. Well, over time I began to grow weary with the "missed" opportunities and the temptation of the pretty faces, so I bought into the delusion. "You're only young once!" "Try it!" "Get it behind you . . . develop some skills that you can take into your marriage one day."

Premarital sex is often viewed as part of the normal singles' experience.

So, if you're single, you may be thinking, "I'm not looking to settle down with anyone anytime soon." If that is the case, you should not be in a romantic or sexual relationship, either. When you think about this, it sounds ridiculous to say that you're not ready to commit your life to someone, but you're ready to give that same person the most intimate part of yourself.

As you evaluate your decision about being sexually active, keep in mind that most people claim to be a lot happier with casual sex than they really are. For them, the act of making love is reduced to the same type of sensation as getting drunk or snorting cocaine; it is strictly a physical experience without any relationship attachment at all. Let's face it, after a while the parties, club hopping, bar hopping, and sexual escapades really get old. That's because they're all the same scene but played out in different locations. It all comes down to the entrapment of a seductive delusion where people have bought into the idea that casual sex is "free love" to be explored at will.

> **It all comes down to the entrapment of a seductive delusion where people have bought into the idea that casual sex is "free love" to be explored at will.**

Just like with drugs, a continued abuse of sex leads to overfamiliarity and dulls the sensation of the experience. By the time someone who was so determined to "enjoy his freedom" gets married, he is often impossible to please sexually and doesn't even know why. Think about this. Where do you want to be in ten, twenty, or even fifty years? Do you want to be part of that couple holding hands on the front porch, watching your grandchildren play? Or do you want to be alone with your memories of the dozens of partners you had in your twenties and thirties or even forties?

Moreover, if you want to get married one day, do you really want to bring all those experiences to your wedding bed? Do you want to guarantee yourself and your marriage partner a frustrated sex life because neither of you are satisfied with what you can offer each other? Remember, when you get married, you have effectively said, "This is *the one* that I want to spend the rest of my life with." If you take the time to think about it, that is a very powerful connection. As I mentioned before, this is a precious God-given gift that was made for the union of a husband and wife. It is very easy to cloud the most significant relationship in your life with counterfeit experiences, thereby short-changing the marriage bed. Be patient so that you can enjoy the real thing.

IS IT WRONG FOR EVERYONE?

Many hear about the idea of saving sex for marriage and respond, "Sure, that's great for some people, but I want to live my life differently." *Relativistic ethics* is a view of life that says ethical truths depend on the individuals and groups who subscribe to them. It maintains that there are no moral absolutes; what is sin to one person can be a "meaningful experience" to another.

> **Are you confident with the choices you make about sex? Would you proudly share them with your children, nieces and nephews, or siblings?**

I don't intend to debate philosophy, so I'll be brief. Are you confident with the choices you make about sex? Would you proudly share them with your children, nieces and nephews, or siblings? Do you someday want to marry someone who has made the same types of choices you are making now?

As much as people want to believe that casual sex is harmless, most people are too often ashamed of themselves "the morning after" or when the relationship breaks off. Some will say that the shame that one feels comes from the puritanical roots of our culture. I suggest that the guilt comes from one's conscience, that little voice inside your head that tells you right from wrong. The voice of your conscience is there not to ruin your fun, but to protect you from bad decisions.

Most people who have lost their virginity prior to marriage knew in their hearts that it wasn't right. They knew that giving themselves to another individual without a lifelong commitment was in some sense lying, being dishonest, or selling themselves short. In fact, regardless of their status, many people confess that their first sexual experience was not so great. It is not uncommon for those who wait until marriage to find the first experience with intercourse to be less than they imagined.

But one of the advantages of marriage is that you have a lifetime of communication and discovery of your sexuality with your spouse. There is an innate sense of security in marriage. The fear of being abandoned, misused, or cheated on are minimized greatly because of your lifelong commitment. This is what makes sex in marriage so much more fulfilling.

EXPOSING THE MYTHS ABOUT CONDOMS

At this point, I'd like to briefly address a topic that is a product of casual sex. You'll probably remember hearing a lot about this in sex education class. It's the dreaded topic of STDs. Each year, there are over three million new cases of STDs in teenagers alone.[1] Mistakenly, the use of condoms is widely heralded as the answer to this problem.

However, the gospel of the condom is a common myth. It carries the assertion that using condoms is the best way to have "protected sex." If that is the case, then why do so many millions contract any number of diseases every year? You've also probably heard that they don't diminish sexual pleasure at all. But, guess what—this isn't true either.

Moreover, it hasn't been properly emphasized that condoms, while fairly effective in preventing pregnancy, were never designed to protect against disease. The natural holes in latex condoms are much larger than viruses, which are just minute pieces of genetic material. It's like trying to keep flies out of your house by putting up chicken wire over your windows—it might help some, but you wouldn't want to rely on it if those flies were carrying a fatal disease.

There are some pretty startling facts surrounding condom use and their effectiveness against the spread of STDs. Here are just a few:

- According to a report entitled *Advance Data from Vital and Health Statistics,* only 19 percent of teen females use condoms.[2]

- According to the Center for Disease Control (CDC), "consistent and correct use of the male latex condom reduces the risk of STD and human immunodeficiency virus (HIV) transmission. However, condom use cannot provide absolute protection against any STD. The most reliable ways to avoid transmission of STDs are to abstain from sexual activity or to be in a long-term mutually monogamous relationship with an uninfected partner."[3]

- When they are being used, condoms must be used consistently and correctly in order for them to be effective. The American Academy of Pediatrics reports, "problems with inconsistent use, incorrect use, breakage, and leakage clearly indicate that condoms cannot be 100 percent effective in preventing pregnancy, STDs, and HIV infection."[4]

- While contraceptives have proven to have some success against HIV/AIDS, their effectiveness in combating other STDs is marginally effective. The CDC provides the following information: "Epidemiologic studies that compare infection rates among condom users and nonusers provide evidence that latex condoms provide limited protection against syphilis and herpes simplex virus-2 [HSV2] transmission."[5]

- The CDC also reports that "chlamydia is the most frequently reported bacterial sexually transmitted disease in the United States. In 2006, 1,030,911 chlamydial infections were reported to CDC from fifty states and the District of Columbia. Under reporting is substantial because most people with chlamydia are not aware of their infections and do not seek testing."[6]

- Further CDC reporting indicates "results of a nationally representative study show that genital herpes infection is common in the United States. Nationwide, at least 45 million people ages 12 and older, or one out of five adolescents and adults, have had genital herpes simplex virus (HSV) infection."[7]

- The Independent Women's Forum (IWF) is an educational institute that focuses on researching issues that concern women, men, and families. It describes the serious nature of another STD and reports some startling news. "HPV (human papillomavirus), a sexually transmitted virus, is the cause of virtually all cervical cancer. The virus is present in 99.7 percent of all cervical cancers according to a study published last year in *The Journal of Pathology*."

The IWF further states, "at least 24 million Americans are infected by HPV according to the National Cancer Institute (NCI). Yet no one knows the true size of the epidemic because, unlike fifty-eight other diseases, the Centers for Disease Control and Prevention (CDC) does not monitor or require case reports of HPV."

Moreover, the IWF reports that the situation is dramatically worsened because "many sexually active Americans think that using a condom can protect them; this is not the case with HPV. According to the NCI, the evidence that condoms do not protect against HPV is so definitive that 'additional research efforts by NCI on the effectiveness of condoms in preventing HPV transmission is not warranted.'"[8]

Did you notice how chlamydia, HSV2, and HPV— the three STDs against which condoms have minimal effect—have become three of the most prevalent STDs? Hmmm . . . It makes one think that, if condoms are so risky when it comes to preventing disease, why have they been highlighted as being so effective?

Unfortunately, campaigns for sexual education awareness do not approach the subject by promoting self-control and abstinence. In choosing to stress condom use, the mindset is that people are going to have sex, so proponents emphasize the use of condoms as a viable option to curtail the spread of disease and unwanted pregnancies.

In addition, most adults received their initial sexual education in high school. However, in the approach utilized in the school environment, there is a glaring omission. By attempting to only deal with the biological aspects of sex in the "value neutral" public school system, in effect, educators misguidedly view human behavior and reduce it to an animalistic activity.

> **Many people become romantically involved with someone simply out of boredom or because they are insecure in being alone.**

By ignoring the emotional and spiritual risks of uncommitted sex and failing to bring awareness to these two important aspects of human nature, the educational system is doing students a tremendous disservice. Although it is true that the risk of STDs is a very real physical danger of extramarital or premarital sex, the emotional and spiritual dangers are just as real.

DATING OR COURTING?

We live in a society where few individuals among the population of singles are satisfied or fulfilled. Many people become romantically involved with someone simply out of boredom or because they are insecure in being alone. While it is a completely natural reaction, the need to feel loved by someone can also be quite dangerous if you allow your identity and happiness to be solely determined by whether you have that "special someone" in your life. Some people are so obsessed with finding their "soul mate" that they become consumed with anxiety and loneliness when that search is unsuccessful.

The obsession with having a partner in life to experience fulfillment is a manifestation of lust. It would be difficult for someone in this volatile state to attract the right person for marriage and experience the physical intimacy God intended, because that is not their primary focus. This is why it is imperative for individuals to learn how to be content on their own, before entertaining thoughts of a serious relationship. Otherwise, people wind up with someone who is not right for them simply because that person was willing and available—there will most likely be serious disappointments in this kind of relationship.

Now even if we reach the point of being confident and content on our own, how are we supposed to meet that person we're meant to be with? We've been taught that in order to discover your partner for life, you must date around until you find a promising candidate. This may seem to make sense at first glance, but far too often broken hearts are the outcome when that idea is put into practice.

I believe there is a better approach. I have observed that having friends to hang out with primarily in a group setting is one of the best ways to safely learn about people. In this setting, you can determine who might be a good prospect for marriage. In fact, it is a healthy way in general to relate socially to members of the opposite sex, whether you intend to marry sooner, later, or not at all.

> **Healthy friendships lay the foundation for a good courtship and marriage.**

Healthy friendships lay the foundation for a good courtship and marriage. What do I mean by "courtship"?

(Sounds archaic and backward, right?) Well, I believe this approach accomplishes the goal of finding your life partner without the risks of dating as we typically understand it. Dating may sometimes be character-ized by selfish attitudes during the relationship and painful breakups at the end. Now I realize that tele-vision shows are full of characters who once dated each other and later turned out to be best friends, but how many "good" breakups have you or any of your friends really had?

This is just a suggestion to be careful when dating because people do not always ate with the intention of investing in the relationship; rather, it could be that the other person is looking for short-term benefits. Often a dating relationship focuses on giving only to get something back in return. (After all, why would you give sacrificially to someone if you're not even sure how long you'll be with him or her?)

On the other hand, in a courtship, the intentions of each party are clear. They are investing time and attention into one another to build a relationship with the goal of marriage in mind. The ideal relationship would also have the benefit of supervision by parents, pastors, and/or a trusted stable couple. This would allow the courting couple access to the counsel and advice of someone in a leadership role to guide them in their decision-making process.

I know that this may sound crazy if you believe that your love life is exclusively your own business.

But why would you refuse input from those who care about you? Mature people who have "been there and done that" can offer wisdom and counsel because they've been down the courtship road and learned some things. They can help you set healthy boundaries to protect both of you from getting too close too fast. Then, if a courting couple discovers during the process that they don't want to marry after all, hopefully, they've treated each other with respect and avoided a lot of unnecessary pain.

Prior to meeting my wife, I was involved in two other courtships. I grew tremendously in both experiences. In each of the two cases, the young lady and I shared a level of honesty that led us to conclude that we were not meant to be together. I won't say that there was no pain involved, but it was also quite liberating to know that we made the right decision along with the guidance and feedback of trusted supervision. I can also say with confidence that in both situations, the young ladies received the utmost respect sexually and otherwise.

I know that to many people, the word "abstinence" is not very welcome. But the truth is, abstinence during a courting relationship is a powerful expression of love and respect. It says, "I respect you enough to control my physical desires." It also allows the couple to concentrate on cultivating the other aspects of the relationship that will be crucial to the long-term success of the marriage. These aspects include solid communication skills, mature conflict resolution, and the ability to love and forgive completely—and unconditionally. All of these issues are basic not only to marriage in general, but to an ongoing, fulfilling sex life.

Your decisions regarding dating and sex will inevitably affect your future marriage and how you rear your children.

You are an intelligent individual; you know deep in your heart that you want God's best in your life. Well, life isn't a series of disconnected events; it's a chain of decisions, one leading to the next. Your decisions regarding dating and sex will inevitably affect your future marriage and how you rear your children. As you are either contemplating or already involved in the "dating scene," it is so important to consult God for the proper way to begin the process. If already involved, make sure to consult with Him from this point on. I'm not saying that choosing abstinence and practicing principles of courtship are easy.

They require focus, discipline, self-control, and self-respect. In many instances, they also involve the pain of sacrifice. But if you press through those seasons of pain, you will enter a promised land of great fulfillment. So many times we allow our emotions to guide us into situations that aren't good for us and we have to make sure that we are making decisions that please God. He is not to be fitted into our plans, but consulted before you decide who that person is you want to (or will) get involved with. Give God the chance to direct you to the person who is compatible with you. You may be in the midst of something that you never thought you would be involved in, but it's not too late to turn back. Ask Him to help you move forward and tell you where He would have you go next or what He would have you do. I guarantee that He will be right there to help you. Trust Him and not yourself.

My hope is that singles will be secure enough as individuals to make intelligent, well-reasoned decisions that will lead to a wonderful future. You don't have to make a lot of tragic mistakes in order to learn. Instead, you can successfully lead a single life that you'll be proud to live before God and to tell your sons and daughters about.

3

Always
and Forever

Marriage may seem like an old-fashioned institution to some, but I believe most individuals will confess that they are willing to take the "plunge" at least once. Yet, some of these same people might ask such questions as, "Why should sex be saved for marriage?" "What is it about marriage that makes the physical act of intercourse different emotionally and spiritually?"

Now, to be fair, I know that there are plenty of people in bad marriages out there who are experiencing less than what they'd like to with regards to sex. And unfortunately they have feelings of it not being all that it's meant to be and not just because of the chemistry of two people hitting some roadblocks. So I'm not saying that getting married guarantees anything. What I am saying is that marriage is the only institution that allows you to avoid seductive delusions because it creates a proper framework to experience sex at its best. Let me say to you that in these kinds of situations, it may be best to seek out counseling to figure out what the issues are in your marriage that may be keeping you from communicating the intimacy that you as an individual (even though you are married) are dealing with issues that you can't seem to tell your spouse. Make sure to sit down with each other (one of you has to be the bigger person and lay aside your differences) and discuss attending a few counseling sessions, just to be able to share the things that are in your heart. If you don't know who to turn to ask for help, start by asking a ministry leader or your pastor and follow through from that initial direction for assistance.

THE MEANING OF
TRUE COMMITMENT

Let me clarify one thing: Marriage is different from the "monogamous relationships" that I alluded to in the previous chapter. Lots of people stay together for months or even years, only to eventually break up. Conversely, marriage means one sex partner for life. It does not mean just one partner at a time. It is not just an emotional commitment, but a legally and spiritually binding one. Please understand that God honors marriage. He also knows that there are times in marriage where you will have tough times. Don't be ashamed to allow Him to carry the burden of what you may believe to have gone—or may be going—wrong in your marriage.

> # Marriage means one sex partner for life. It does not mean just one partner at a time.

Before the phenomenon of "no-fault" divorce, a couple who wanted to end their marriage had to prove in court that there was a compelling reason, such as adultery or abandonment. This proof was necessary because being joined together in marriage is the most serious commitment that two people can make with each other. Having a spouse is different from having a roommate. A husband and wife not only join their bodies, but their hearts, goals, and dreams as well. The bond between them forms a new family, and the strength of that bond will determine the strength of that family.

True commitment in a relationship is unconditional and doesn't have time limits. It doesn't say, "I'll be faithful to you as long as the relationship is working for me."

Instead of two people who are pursuing their own separate interests and just happen to live together, married couples are pursuing joint goals. Moreover, their children become part of the team to accomplish those goals. Individuals are strengthened when they know that they are part of a solid family who will celebrate with them when times are good and support them in times of need. The strength of that family comes from the commitment of the husband and wife to one another.

True commitment in a relationship is unconditional and doesn't have time limits. It doesn't say, "I'll be faithful to you as long as the relationship is working for me." Nor does it say, "Let's give this a try for a year." That's why true commitments aren't made without careful consideration beforehand. Its what we talked about in chapter 1. Love is unconditional and you are loved just because you're—you.

The lack of depth found in most boyfriend/ girlfriend relationships is demonstrated by how easily people get in and out of them. When the fun wears off or when life seems to take a new direction, it's over. It is this mentality and practice that has been a major factor in many failing marriages. No matter how comfortable it may feel at a given time, non-marital /courtship romances are unstable, and an unstable relationship is no place for sex. I can't stress enough how important it is to lay a foundation for friendship in relationships. The stability of any relationship comes from the foundation. Take the time to get it right by making the best decisions possible.

THE RELATIONSHIP MAKES THE SEX

Consider this. Studies actually show that married people who don't cheat have the highest rate of sexual satisfaction when compared to sexually active singles and adulterers. According to *Sex in America: A Definitive Survey,* Robert T. Michael, *et al.,* indicate that, "people who reported being the most physically and emotionally satisfied [sexually] were the married couples."[9] Why is this? How can being with the same person for years and years possibly be more fulfilling physically than any other type of sexual encounter?

Let's look at both sides of the coin. You have people who are married experiencing their sexuality in a lifelong commitment that creates a depth beyond comparison. Then again, you have people who, whether married or single, indulge in short-term sexual en-counters with multiple partners over a period of time. What kinds of people indulge in sex as singles or commit adultery in marriage? The kind of people who are hurting and unfulfilled—not just sexually—but emotionally and spiritually.

Could it be that the type of people who are con-tent as individuals and secure on their own are the type who abstain until marriage and stay faithful afterward? On the other hand, could it also be that an exclusive sexual relationship for life isn't as dull and boring as pop culture makes it out to be? Cou-ples who really love each other have a lifetime to dis-cover their partners on all levels, including learning how to please each other physically.

Let's not forget that sex is very powerful. There is an incredible bond that takes place when two people have intercourse. This powerful exchange creates a union that is not to be violated, because it is the for-mation of a lifelong commitment that should be in place prior to the act of intercourse. Therefore, it is a spiritual event because the Creator made it that way. In other words, sex should be the culmination or celebration of the wedding vows made between a man and a woman. From that point on, it's all about exploration and discovery!

Couples who really love each other have a lifetime to discover their partners on all levels, including learning how to please each other physically.

This process of discovery can be one of the most exciting elements of a relationship. While there still remains some anxiety of wanting to make a good first impression in bed with a new partner, the plus side is that you don't only get one chance to prove your prowess, because it's not a one-night stand. So for married couples, if there weren't fireworks tonight, hopefully nobody feels insecure about it, because there's always tomorrow.

Furthermore, disease, out-of-wedlock pregnancy, and guilt aren't there to pollute the environment. In addition, married couples get to "make love all day long," not literally, but through the environment they create in their home. They can build up such a love and trust for one another that the physical act of love-making is only one natural component of an ongoing spiritual and emotional intimacy.

WHY CAN'T WE LIVE TOGETHER FIRST?

You have probably guessed it by now. I don't believe that people should live together. However, I do want to address it briefly. Non-marital cohabitation (the technical term) is still illegal in most states, but nonetheless it has become a fairly common practice. Some even do it with the blessing of their parents, while others would panic at an unannounced visit from Mom.

Although I don't advocate that platonic friends of the opposite sex be roommates, even with separate bedrooms, I'm specifically talking here about people who want to live together with the intention of possibly getting married later. Their reasoning is that by trying a live-in relationship first, they'll know better if their partner is the right person with whom to spend the rest of their life. As logical as it may sound, studies show that it doesn't work.

David Popenoe, a professor of sociology at Rutgers University, presents findings from a study conducted by the National Marriage Project, where he is codirector. The study showed that divorce rates are even higher for those who cohabitate before marriage. The evidence seems to show that living together before marriage increases the risk of divorce. His research debunks the myth that living together before marriage is a good way to reduce the chances of eventually divorcing.

Popenoe states, "Many studies have found that those who live together before marriage have a considerably higher chance of eventually divorcing. The reasons for this are not well understood. In part, the type of people who are willing to cohabit may also be those who are more willing to divorce. There is some evidence that the act of cohabitation itself generates attitudes in people that are more conducive to divorce, for example, the attitude that relationships are temporary and easily can be ended."[10]

Hey, maybe the best start for a marriage is that old-fashioned courtship we talked about in the last chapter. I've thrown a lot at you in only a few chapters, but I implore you to consider the facts, figures, and opinions you've read and give courtship a try. What do you have to lose? I contend that you have everything to gain. That's always the case when you do things God's way.

Commitment to abstinence before marriage was one of the greatest decisions that I ever made. It prepared me in the art of making love to my wife. Why?

Prior to marriage, I learned how to make love to her heart and mind, which eventually prepared the ground for our wedding night. The energies that would otherwise be expressed sexually were first expressed in other meaningful ways. Whether by the prayers, gifts, words of affection, or acts of service that I offered on her behalf, I respected my wife's virtue.

My wife often shares the fact that I never violated her, which made her feel safe and secure. As a result, through the rich intimacy and powerful bond that we share, she has shown me how much she appreciates my efforts to please her. I directed my energies through communicating my love and affection for her without being sexual. This approach was great in winning her, and I continue to show her the same level of care and attention now that we are married. It has proven to be extremely satisfactory in keeping her from feeling used as a sexual toy to meet my needs.

I do caution individuals about "when" and "how" they should express loving acts prior to marriage. The end result can build emotions that they will eventually desire to express sexually. It would be very naïve to think otherwise. The amount of time you spend on the phone, hanging out together alone, lovingly touching, exchanging words of affection—these are all extremely effective stimulators. They play a part in building intimacy. Unless you are a creature from another planet, physical and intimate contact will build the desire to express your emotions in a physical way. Eventually, this activity either leads to sex or extreme sexual frustration!

So, be prayerfully patient in the process of building spiritual and emotional intimacy. I recommend a good book to use as a guide for the various phases in a relationship. It is entitled *Choosing God's Best: Wisdom for Lifelong Romance* and was written by Dr. Don Raunikar.[11]

Y**ou can begin assigning value to tomorrow's marriage with the choices that you make today.**

I realize that, to some people, all this marriage talk sounds not only like this information is not for singles, but is also a bit archaic—and impossible to fulfill. So even if one agrees that sex is best when saved for marriage, he or she might still wonder, is it worth the seemingly high price of waiting? My answer is yes, it's worth it. You are worth it. Your future spouse is worth it. You can begin assigning value to tomorrow's marriage with the choices that you make today. You may ask, "How do I get to the place of finding that one person to whom I will commit the rest of my life?" For example, you might ask, "Don't I have to go to various restaurants to determine the different tastes that I enjoy? Well, why isn't a similar process applicable when choosing the opposite sex?" Your point is well taken, but know that your first priority should be one of self-discovery.

Consider this as well. I've mentioned beginning a relationship on a good foundation a time or two previously, and a good way to do that is by making sure to approach relationships through friendship. Your friends are your buddies, correct? You'd do anything in the world for your friends, correct? You'd never consider ever hurting any of your friends, correct? Well, if you are ever considering getting married one day, you will need to have established a friendship with the person you are in a relationship with to achieve the level of trust and respect that can never be lost. Friends are forever! You have to admit that at least it's a good place to start.

WHO ARE YOU?

You can't expect someone else to love you effectively if you don't love yourself. Nor can you adequately communicate how you are to be loved. This fact could explain why there might be ongoing frustration for you. Mere companionship with another individual does not satisfy that deep longing within. If you haven't learned to love yourself, you will wind up with the short end of the stick.

> **It stands to reason that the best person to teach you about yourself is the One who created you.**

There is something that we must all understand and come to grips with: We cannot leave this one vital element out of the equation. In order to love yourself effectively, it is important to enter into a reality of how the Creator loves you. And to do that, the first intimate relationship in your life must be with God. As we know, an intimate relationship of course requires you to spend time with the person you love. Spend time with God and get to know Him. He's waiting to answer all of your questions and love you, through the pain of you discovering what He already knows about you. We all have issues and situations that God wants to rescue us from, but rescue can only come when we surrender our hearts to Him and allow His best for us. It stands to reason that the best person to teach you about yourself is the One who created you. The One who knows all your quirks and intricacies is equipped to provide you with the supportive relationships you need to meet your emotional needs.

He will establish you and help you discover who you are. Once you are on a firm foundation and secure within yourself, He will lead you to acquire your full inheritance—including the lovely bride or wonderful groom that He created just for you. But remember this: If you are to be successful in finding that person, it is of the utmost importance that you first focus on the kind of bride or groom you will be, one who is whole and completely satisfied with yourself and God.

The Power
of Purity

Because sex at its best requires intimacy on the spiritual, physical, and emotional levels, anything less would mean that people are simply engaging in seductive delusions. These delusions can lead you to unknown and unwanted paths that can cause more pain than you ever expected or were already involved in. The spiritual aspect of sex exists because God Himself created the institution of marriage and intends for it to be a relationship that endures for a lifetime. And, within it, He established the act of physical intimacy and sexual bonding to be a permanent fixture.

That is why true sexual fulfillment is an emotional experience that can only be achieved through an intense vulnerability shared with another person through the mutual, lifelong commitment known as marriage. The bond between a husband and wife embodies the most significant relationship that can be experienced between a man and a woman.

The foundational pillars of commitment, intimacy, and fulfillment define the marital relationship. As boundaries, they are directly related to sex within the context of marriage and are reserved for married couples only. On the other hand, outside of the framework of marriage, the boundary of sex is not designed to be detrimental or a trap to individuals; rather, it is intended to be beneficial. As single people rightly regard sex and save it for the sanctity of marriage, they will not get caught up in seductive delusions that only prove to be painful and destructive. Isn't that the point? Don't you want to avoid the pitfalls and traps that await you when you stray from what God has for you, the person whom God has for you? Furthermore, I have attempted to refute the false notion that views tolerance of promiscuity and extramarital sex as more enlightened ways of thinking than practicing abstinence.

The following is yet another way in which the human sex life can become polluted, often without an unsuspecting person even realizing it.

THE HIDDEN ENEMY

Pornography has been around for thousands of years in various forms, but I am grieved to see its widespread growth and acceptance in contemporary times. When it comes to sexually explicit materials, women are valued strictly for their external appearance and skill in providing sexual performances. The tools of seduction further contain a blatant message that is difficult to overlook: Once a woman's youthful beauty fades, so does her worth.

I define pornography as *any mental or visual stimuli that would entice an individual to lust or fantasize.*

Unfortunately, the media has played a major role in the widespread acceptance of this dehumanizing attitude, because these practices effectively sell related products and programs. And women aren't the only losers in the equation. With continual exposure to pornographic materials, men become conditioned to respond to their basest instincts.

Let me also say that I'm not just referring to XXX-rated movies and magazines. I define pornography as *any mental or visual stimuli that would entice an individual to lust or fantasize.* You don't have to agree with this definition, but I think you'll find that pornographic innuendos can be seen and felt in advertisements, literature, soap operas, music videos, radio, and almost any other form of communication.

Even so, many people believe that sexually suggestive material, including the more hard-core stuff, is harmless. After all, you're not actually *with* the person, right? No risk of STDs or pregnancy is present. Also, there's no involvement of that emotionally damaging relationship stuff that I've been talking about. I disagree. True, the physical dangers are eliminated with pornography. But considering the emotional element that is also involved, it is still a breeding ground for insatiable lust. When you subscribe to it, that hunger will always have you searching for more.

Do you know anyone who was lonely and found lasting comfort in a magazine? Do insecure people really gain confidence and hope from watching pornography? Yet even as empty and pathetic as the whole "porn experience" may be, there is an even deeper danger. Your greatest sexual organ is your mind. The adage, "You are what you eat," is true about a lot of things. Feeding your mind with various kinds of pornographic activity is actually a toxic source of deception. Pornography distorts reality and results in seductive delusions that are harmful to one's wellbeing. For example, if my perception of women is defined by the strip clubbin', shakin' yo' thang, street pimpin' images that I see in various media, than

It is not possible to take in an image visually, enjoy it for a few moments, and then expect that it will leave the mind and heart unaffected.

whether I should or shouldn't, I would relate to women in that way. I would be living in a fantasy world and gradually alienating myself from genuine intimate relationships. It is not possible to take in an image visually, enjoy it for a few moments, and then expect that it will leave the mind and heart unaffected. Anyone who thinks that they can escape from this outcome is merely engaging in seductive delusions.

I mentioned earlier that promiscuity will dull the sexual experience over time for people in the same manner that a drug addict becomes tolerant to his drug of choice. Pornography is the same way. Furthermore, by its very nature, it sends the message that sex must be dirty or nasty to be enjoyable. The more you read or view, the cruder that material has to be so that it can achieve the desired level of response.

This is a subtle process that occurs over time, but many who start in their teens may find that by the time they reach their thirties, normal sex simply doesn't "do it for them" anymore.

Even if a person has not gone off the deep end with pornography, the habit of allowing one's mind to develop sexual fantasies is the basis for major physical disappointments and emotional trouble. Anyone who has been sexually active and is honest about it will tell you that their actual experiences never equal what they have imagined in their minds. Isn't it strange how we can chase after an illusion of happiness only to later find out that it wasn't all that we thought it would be?

For example, I am aware of several situations where either the husband or wife decided to indulge in an adulterous relationship because he or she was dissatisfied in the marriage. Part of the dissatisfaction was clearly driven by delusions of sexual fantasies. The cheating spouse bought into the notion that there was more excitement and pleasure to be found outside of the marriage rather than within. Unfortunately, when that spouse awakened from his or her delusion (which doesn't always happen), the damage done to the marriage and all who are connected to that couple (children, family, friends) was irreparable.

Sexual fantasies and everything that feeds them (music, videos, movies, magazines, explicit romance novels, soap operas, and so on) are the primary sources of improper sexual behavior and are driven by nothing more than seductive delusions.

WHO DO YOU BELONG TO?

This is a good question to ask yourself, because the answer will determine if you are a child of God. How you answer the question can also give you an opportunity to check up on yourself and how well you are coping with life. My point is that ongoing personal improvement should be the goal and we can always try to do better. But the question also gets at a deeper meaning, because the answer lies at the very core of our motivation for the things that we do.

The truth is, for the children of God, we have a different standard. There is a better way for us to live because our lifestyle directly relates to who we are in His eyes. How do you look at yourself? Do you focus on and place priority on your own selfish needs and desires? Or do you realize that you weren't put on this earth to fulfill your own self-seeking objectives?

We do have a choice. But before you settle on the latter, consider the following passage from God's Word. Remember, God made us; we didn't make ourselves. And He had a definite reason in mind when He did. So, while you're checking this out, think about what it really means to you and how you can apply it to your daily life. Maybe you just might need to make some practical changes in light of the message that God is sending here.

All things are lawful for me, but
not all things are profitable. All things are
lawful for me, but I will not
be mastered by anything.
Food is for the stomach and the stomach is
for food, but God will do away with both of
them. Yet the body is not for immorality, but
for the Lord, and the Lord is for the body.
Now God has not only raised the
Lord, but will also raise us up
through His power.
Do you not know that your bodies are
members of Christ? Shall I then take away
the members of Christ and make them
members of a prostitute?
May it never be!
Or do you not know that the one who joins
himself to a prostitute is one
body with her? For He says,
"THE TWO SHALL BECOME ONE FLESH."
But the one who joins himself to
the Lord is one spirit with Him.
Flee immorality. Every other *sin that a man*
commits is outside the body, but the immoral
man sins against his own body.

Or do you not know that your body is a
temple of the Holy Spirit who is in you,
whom you have from God, and that
you are not your own?
For you have been bought with a price:
therefore glorify God in your body.
—1 Corinthians 6:12–20

The writer, the apostle Paul, is trying to tell us that we have the freedom to choose. But because of our salvation in Christ, he wants us to think really hard about the choices that we make. We may not want to do everything that we are free to do, simply because we can. And that definitely includes sexual impurity.

Anyone who believes that it's okay to have sex outside of marriage will disagree. An individual might override God's will and use his or her freedom in Christ as a ticket to justify his or her behavior, but it is not a free pass with which to commit sin. Actually, that reasoning will keep a person oppressed by sin. God has given us the power to live a life of purity.

You see, when we choose Christ, we become part of Him. He gave up His life for us, and that sealed the deal. He saved us from sin and death, and we received the power of God with all the fringe benefits. You might think of it as having a secret weapon that you once did not have but now you can use to fight against temptation.

So, what do you think? If you accept the fact that

your body is a member of Christ's body, do you treat it that way? Are the choices you are making pleasing in God's eyes? What kind of choices are you making that may be preventing you from experiencing God's best?

Living free from lust and perversion is very possible and very liberating.

PURITY AS A LIFESTYLE

Although I was successful at avoiding premarital sexual contact since the time of my youth, walking in purity has been an ongoing journey for me. I have experienced many battles with victories and defeats. But at the end of the day, I can say that living free from lust and perversion is very possible and very liberating. A lifestyle of purity is more than just saving intercourse for marriage. It is a commitment to the pursuit of having a pure mind, spirit, and body.

I can clearly remember my first night away from home on a college campus, where the true test of my decision to remain pure was staring me in my face. I had already been practicing abstinence for two years in high school. While that was a great achievement, there were enough support and boundaries around me to effectively reduce the opportunity for any sexual encounters.

However, once I arrived at the University of Maryland at College Park, I was immediately put to the test and had to prove my determination. Freshmen had to check in early for orientation prior to classes. Since my roommate was a sophomore, I had the room to myself for about four days. Now let me remind you, before I decided to practice abstinence, I knew that when I got to college, I would be in hot pursuit to keep "female company."

So, here's the scenario. I was on a beautiful college campus, outnumbered by young women, at least three-to-one. It was going to be huge for me not to pursue any sexual relationships—borderline miraculous. But the decision that I had made was real. The love of God that I encountered was real. Even so, I remember how I cried that first night. Everything in my lower nature wanted to exploit the so-called "opportunity" to have female companionship.

After all, I was away from home and the watchful eyes of parental supervision. I was in my room alone—no one would know except me and a consenting young lady. Yet, that wasn't really the whole story. Someone else would know, and He was the One who ultimately counted.

I believe that knowledge of God's presence was the

thing that actually kept me grounded. The tears finally stopped when this awareness helped me to succeed in shaking off the immediate delusion that I was struggling with. What else would have motivated me to pick up my Bible and read the following scripture?

> *Therefore, since we have so great a cloud of witnesses surrounding us, let us also lay aside every encumbrance and the sin which so easily entangles us, and let us run with endurance the race that is set before us, fixing our eyes on Jesus, the author and perfecter of faith, who for the joy set before Him endured the cross, despising the shame, and has sat down at the right hand of the throne of God. For consider Him who has endured such hostility by sinners against Himself, so that you will not grow weary and lose heart. You have not yet resisted to the point of shedding blood in your striving against sin."*
> —Hebrews 12:1–4

The message that really broke me was found in the last verse. It bears repeating: *You have not yet resisted to the point of shedding blood in your striving against sin.* Even though my choice that night to deny my sexual urges was painful to me, it didn't require any bloodshed on my part. This insight brought incredible peace and comfort to my mind, will, and emotions. It also laid a solid foundation for the next four years of my efforts to remain pure in college.

In fact, the words of Scripture helped to keep me on the right track for the rest of my single days. During our engagement, one of the most precious memories that I cherish is a rare occasion alone with my future wife. We were less than sixty days away from getting married, and the emotional desires for physical affection were ever increasing.

When you commit to purity, you are inviting almighty God into your daily experience.

The setup for sexual intimacy was ideal. It was late in the afternoon. We had spent the morning running errands in preparation for the wedding and had taken a nice stroll in the park. Afterward, we were lounging on the sofa, enjoying the coziness of the moment. Instead of taking that opportunity for physical intimacy, I chose to read the scriptures while she fell asleep close to me.

She felt safe and comfortable lying on me without any fear or pressure from me to have sex. It was good to know that in the midst of an intimate time with my fiancée, I had no desire to have sex. I can honestly say that because God is love and God is pure—love is pure. That day typified the purity we experienced in our relationship. It will be something that we'll treasure for the rest of our lives.

Isn't life so much better when you aren't ashamed of your thoughts and actions?

Jesus said, *"Blessed are the pure in heart, for they shall see God,"* (Matthew 5:8). When you commit to purity, you are inviting almighty God into your daily experience. The mindset then becomes one of accountability when you say, "I am married to God, and I will not do anything to bring separation in my relationship with Him." I actually shudder at the idea of my devotion and desire being given to another woman apart from my wife. That would essentially rob her of what she deserves. In learning how to focus my emotions toward heaven prior to marriage, I was able to release them "when the time came." Then I could give my all to my wife—who is God's precious gift in my life.

Sexually explicit programs and materials are exploitations, not celebrations, of human sexuality. Avoiding such things does not mean that you believe sexual desire is wrong. On the contrary, it is because sex is so pure and sacred that I choose to turn away from stuff that tries to reduce it to a meaningless animal instinct.

Having a pure heart is a wonderful thing. Don't you feel good when your conscience is clean? Doesn't it make your heart full of joy when you know God is smiling on you? Isn't life so much better when you aren't ashamed of your thoughts and actions? It is this kind of purity that is the starting point for true intimacy in relationships. A focus on purity leads to the rejection of seductive delusions—and builds a foundation for a fulfilling sex life. The life of purity can be achieved one step at a time by keeping the Word of God the center of your life and seeking His face for each decision you make.

Start today. Don't allow your past mistakes to stop you from experiencing the peace of mind that I've been talking about throughout this book. The beauty of starting today is that you will be able to begin to have the heaviness of the cloud that has been overhead move its way—away from you. If you are in Christ and you recall experiencing His wonderful grace and mercy, know that it is available to you today too! If you are not in Christ and don't know what it's like to be comforted by the Holy Spirit, you can reach out to Him right now! When you turn toward Him and ask for His guidance to help you reach out to Christ, He will consume you with His love and power of forgiveness. This, my friend, is the ultimate experience you've been waiting for. So don't delay; begin your journey. It's well worth it!

5

A Letter to My Sisters

Dear Sisters,

Over the years, I have met many of you who have expressed your frustration and discouragement concerning relationships. It seems to be very difficult to meet a guy who has the strength and sensitivity that you need and desire. The issue of sex almost always comes up, and typically the brother doesn't want to continue a relationship without it.

After experiencing this disappointment repeatedly, the process of self-examination starts to kick in. Questions arise like, "What is wrong with me?" "Will things ever change?" "Am I worth it?" "Why doesn't anybody want to love me?"

FIRST THINGS FIRST

Sisters, please know this. On behalf of every brother who has lied to you, on behalf of every brother who has deceived you, on behalf of every brother who has abused you physically, mentally, and spiritually— I am sorry. I personally feel compelled to apologize for the lies, deceptions, insensitivities, cheating, and abuse that you all have collectively endured.

The issue of sex almost always comes up, and typically the brother doesn't want to continue a relationship without it.

Many men have been a gross misrepresentation of how a woman is supposed to be treated and honored. In the absence of your fathers, we thought that we could treat you like peasants instead of princesses. We were blind to the reality and necessity of respecting you as one of God's treasures from heaven.

A Letter to My Sisters

Please forgive us for not entering into the fullness of our masculinity. And in that masculinity is where we express our utmost respect for your well-being with honesty, courtesy, patience, and protection (to name a few). Please forgive us for becoming paralyzed in puberty and not growing into the men whom God expects us to be. You see, men equate love with sex, meaning, we only *play* at the idea of love to get sex. We have rejected responsibility and commitment, both of which indicate the measure of our masculinity. Let me confess to you—we must change. And I pray by the grace of God that we will change. I make no excuses in also asking that you pray for us as well. Pray that when we encounter our sisters in Christ that we will treat them with brotherly love. This is something that most of us have been taught, but in which we still need some guidance. And for those of us who haven't been taught pray that you are guided by God to not be lead by the nurturer that has been put in you to "rescue" us from our situation, but that God would create a work in us that is life-changing, for us to give and show His best.

In light of acknowledging our own issues as men, there are some words regarding your need for intimacy and relationships that I would like to leave with you, my sisters.

FINDING YOUR BALANCE

There are three dimensions of you where truth must reign in your life. You are spirit, soul (mental and emotional), and body. I believe that when you focus on developing your spiritual self, the mental, emotional, and physical will all come into alignment. At the same time, you cannot truly focus on one characteristic of your being and forsake the other aspects of who you are. If you try to live this way, then it will lead to an unbalanced life and that is not God's best for you.

> **It is important to embrace how God sees you.**

In many instances, it is human nature to place emphasis on keeping the physical, emotional, and mental self together. But the spiritual self is too often treated as an afterthought. In that case, God doesn't receive any quality time from you. He only gets the attention that is left over in your busy life. When I suggest that you focus on your spiritual self, I mean that it is important to embrace how God sees you. He wants to be in a relationship with you, but it takes work—just like being in any other relationship. Hey, don't always be so hard on yourself. It's so easy to put more pressure on yourself than you should. Nobody's perfect. Otherwise, we wouldn't need or depend on God for anything. But because He won't force His will on us, we sometimes feel that He isn't near. On the contrary, God is always there to walk you through life's twists and turns. He tells us in His Word that He will never leave us or forsake us. He will even pick up the shattered pieces that you either give to Him or step back and allow Him to fix for you. It first takes having a heart of surrender, which will keep you humble and welcome His ever-present love and care for you.

You are incredibly special in His eyes and He will truly be the Lover of your soul, if you only believe. The key is to make yourself available to Him so that God can reveal Himself to you in deeper dimensions. Quiet walks in the park, special gifts given, and loving words exchanged in the middle of the night are all experiences that the Lord wants to bring into your world. There is a spiritual ecstasy that will spread satisfaction through-out your total being. But it must begin with you walk-ing in an awareness and acceptance of the truth about you and the One who created you.

This ongoing process of spiritual development will totally impact how you will allow yourself to be treated. To the degree that you have self-respect and self-worth, you will automatically command it from others. Once you realize that you are a "pearl of great price," you won't allow a brother to treat you like you are on sale at the clearance counter. It seems like far too often the cry for emotional comfort causes a woman to settle for less than what God has intended. I pray that you will find the time and energy to nurture a sweet communion with heaven. Spending time with your heavenly Father will protect you from having ungodly relationships on earth. It's so worth it! Try it and see. He's waiting for you.

> **Once you realize that you are a "pearl of great price," you won't allow a brother to treat you like you are on sale at the clearance counter.**

A FINAL MESSAGE

It can be difficult interacting with the opposite sex on a platonic level because of human nature. Without creating proper boundaries, it is easy to get emotionally attached without even engaging in sex. My heart goes out to you ladies who have endured a lot of foolishness from men. And because of it, I know some of you may have become bitter and unforgiving. Don't allow those bad situations with that kind of man to discourage you or stop you from giving God the chance, to heal your heart. Again, He sees you and knows what you need. Give God a chance and you won't have to worry about your troubled past. Furthermore, I am fully convinced that if you commit your way to searching for genuine truth in all that you do, the potential for you to find true love and fulfillment is unlimited. Invest in yourself spiritually, mentally, emotionally, and physically. Pursue those goals, dreams, and ambitions that you carry in your heart.

Don't wait on male companionship or the prospect of marriage to pursue your dreams. What if you never get married? Are you comfortable with that? Have you made sure to consider it as an option? If not, are you open to marrying outside of your race? These and other questions like the ones asked are what you need to grapple with to discover the answers. Ask God to help you search within yourself and find out what you really need to make you whole. Always remember what the Word of God tells you to do:

Seductive Delusions

*Trust in the Lord with all your heart, and
lean not on your own understanding; In all
your ways acknowledge Him, And He shall
direct your paths.*
—Proverbs 3:5–6 NKJV

Now I realize there will be moments where you
don't feel like trusting, acknowledging, or confessing
anything! You want to be held, spoken to softly, and
treated like a queen. This is the time when you are
most vulnerable and need your close friends, parents,
or parental figures to connect with so that they can
provide you with some TLC (tender loving care).
Ladies, so many times you have been placed in the
role of having to take care of just about everything
(i.e. paying all the bills, taking care of the children,
working long hours, cleaning, cooking, getting the car
repaired, etc.) that you begin to feel as though there
is no one who is going to help you. You retreat from
life and don't allow others in who are waiting in the
wings to assist you. Try your best to lighten your load
by seeking out those you trust to come to your aid.
Even if it means you only share your burden with
someone who will at least pray for you (which of
course is the driving force for finding the strength),
you need to continue your everyday pursuits.

As well, if you seize the moment, this would also
be the opportune time to increase your level of intimacy with the Lover of your soul—Jesus. You can

trust Him. Jesus will meet you at your point of need. He will become more real and satisfying to you in your moments of transparency, if you take the time to acknowledge Him. And remember, He promises to direct your paths. Putting forth the effort is critical to your well-being. Who knows? Maybe without even bumping into the right brother along the way, just maybe you will figure out that the assistance and fulfillment you have been looking for all this time is right there in Christ. He's waiting on you to come to Him with every little bit of burden you have. Yeah, even that one! The one that you think is so insignificant that God couldn't possibly care about it. His grace is sufficient for you!

> **You can trust Him.
> Jesus will meet you
> at your point of need.**

6

A Letter to My Brothers

Dear Brothers,

There is an enemy out to steal, kill, and destroy your divine inheritance. Brother, that enemy has been plotting against you for multiple generations, not wanting you to flourish in your relationships with your Creator, your friends, your family, and everyone whom you meet. He cleverly disguises himself as your friend, your partner, one of your boys, the one who's "got your back."

This so-called friend teaches you to be self-serving and self-centered—the god of your world. He persuades you to pacify your pains, fears, and worries with momentary comforts such as alcohol, drugs, pornography, sex, prostitution, arrogance, male chauvinism, and many other destructive behaviors. These detrimental activities are marketed to help you "cope" with the weight that you carry on a daily basis.

> **There is an enemy out to steal, kill, and destroy your divine inheritance.**

But, in actuality, this "friend" is your archenemy who discourages you from growing in attributes such as honesty and integrity, commitment and responsibility, loyalty and devotion, humility and self-control. Lust is his name, and he knows that your role as a future or current husband and father are keys to a stable society that would make it extremely difficult for him to survive. Therefore, he has systematically attempted to weave into your psyche habits and patterns that are contrary to true love and godliness. It would behoove you not to listen to and/or give in to this great temptation.

God is constantly calling men to live a holy and complete life in Him. Answer the call, and continue to seek God's face to keep you, on the straight and narrow path that He has laid out for you to follow Him in all His righteousness. He tells us in His Word that

He is your way of escape. But you can't escape if you're not looking for an exit. Look for Him to show you the way out! It is imperative that you remember that you were formed in His image and your leadership, or lack thereof, will determine whether the many lives you touch will grow in Christ or seek out the world for its opinion of who they are supposed to be.

Our divine inheritance is to be a visible expression of God in the earth. Our Creator has designed an excellent plan for us to experience His best for our lives in every way. When the plan is operating because we have set our hearts and minds to making it work, God's intention is for women to come in contact with us and know that they have experienced a measure of God. When children come in contact with us, they will know that they have experienced a measure of God. When the elderly come in contact with us, they too will know they that have experienced a measure of God.

This by no means implies that we are perfect and possess no character flaws. However, it does mean that we have a standard by which our lives are governed, and that standard provokes us to continuously grow and develop on a higher plane. God created the man first and made us the leader for a reason. Some of you may even be thinking that this is how it was supposed to be. That of course God chose the man to be the leader. We cannot fully understand why; He could have designed a different plan and made the opposite sex first—but He didn't. So don't allow chauvinistic attitudes to govern the way you think with regard to your leadership role.

> # Our divine inheritance is to be a visible expression of God in the earth.

All we know is that He is an excellent God and His ways supersede all others. Ours is not to question God's motives. We are simply to obey His commands. After God made the man and then the woman, the Bible describes the fundamental purpose of the relationship between the two beings.

> *For this reason a man shall leave*
> *his father and his mother, and be joined to*
> *his wife; and they shall become one flesh.*
> —Genesis 2:24

This is what God intended from the very beginning. He smiled upon His creation and blessed it to prosper. When we approach life and do things God's way, He is pleased and we get all the benefits that He has for us. Don't miss out on everything that God has for you by turning your back on God to do things your way. His authority supersedes the authority He has given us, and we better make sure to walk in the path He presents to us. That way we can bypass the potholes in the road that the devil so desperately wants us to fall into. Through the process of living life as God expects us to, we will experience more of God's likeness spilling into our daily affairs.

So how does this apply to us sexually? Since we carry the sperm that gives life, we must understand the responsibility associated with sexual intercourse. It is irresponsible to be sexually intimate with a woman you have not committed your life to within the bond of marriage. To function in her God-given role, a woman needs safety and security, and a lifelong commitment from a devoted brother who helps to ensure that she is safe and secure. Keep your mind clear of distasteful images of women so that when and if a situation occurs that may harm your sister in Christ, you will have a better chance of taking the high road and not violating her in any way. Isn't that what God wants for your life? Don't you want to be a pleaser of God and not a pleaser of this world?

To enjoy a woman merely for personal pleasure before you commit the rest of your life to her is self-serving and shortsighted. Selfish actions create the wrong foundation for a relationship, ultimately creating emotional and spiritual problems—if not physical problems as well. Maybe it won't affect you directly, but the next brother who is introduced to her life will have to swim through the muddy waters of her heart that you have soiled. To that end, a vicious cycle continues when this repeatedly happens. This unfortunate cycle creates unstable relationships that, in turn, produce unstable families that, in turn, create unstable communities, and so on.

> Through the process of living life as God expects us to, we will experience more of God's likeness spilling into our daily affairs.

Why is there a sense of lawlessness in the land today? Why is there so much anger, hatred, and perversion? Could it be that people are responding out of the pain inflicted by broken homes and broken relationships, which, in some cases, has gone on for generations? The deepest human longing is for genuine love, yet we try to attain it by the principles that govern lust. Robbing someone of what we are called to do within our leadership roles must stop! We can no longer step down from that role (however momentarily it may be) to indulge in the forbidden. These irresponsible acts of vandalism have got to be put in check, and it starts with you. Is this something that is going to be easy? Not at all. But it is something we must do to honor the place that God has designed us to be, and He has put us there for His purpose—not ours!

When we live life for ourselves, seeking momentary pleasures without being willing to take responsibility for the consequences, the results will leave us inwardly unfulfilled. And it will in some cases create a pathway of devastation that is sometimes irreparable. Do you want this to be the legacy that you leave for our future generations? Do you want to live with the weight of this burden? Do you want our women to see us as the predators and beasts that this enemy makes us become? This enemy called lust convinces us to focus on self-gratification at the expense of someone else's well-being. It seems to be much easier to get involved in multiple relationships where the women meet immediate physical and emotional needs, rather than focus our time on nurturing one relationship that has the potential to grow deep and wide. Stop my brothers and think! Think for just one moment of the horrific impression that our women have of us. Doesn't that make you want to do better?

It certainly should. Begin with yourself, and mentor another brother to do the same. Come alongside a younger brother, and see that he makes better decisions with his life. Encourage him to go after the best life he can achieve in Christ. Don't sit back and watch him make the same mistakes that you have made—or worse. If you've gone down this path or not, make sure another brother doesn't.

> When it comes to male-female relationships and families, men are the leaders and we have a tremendous responsibility to pursue righteousness.

When it comes to male-female relationships and families, men are the leaders and we have a tremendous responsibility to pursue righteousness. Creating a righteous environment builds something that lasts, something that can endure the test of time. Our relationships should begin with a spiritual foundation that informs the mental and emotional dimensions, ultimately leading to the physical expression within the context of marriage. This is the righteousness we are called to pursue. But it cannot happen without knowing the Righteous One. The Bible tells us to seek Him while He may be found. And to call on Him while He's near. That simply means to take the opportunities that He is giving you and to seize your moment! To undo some of the damage that has been done for so long. To find your righteousness in Him. It's available to everyone, but you have to find Him for yourself. Once you do, He will make the difference in you that only He can make. It's not just for show—ask me how I know. He's the real thing. And when you yield totally to Him, you'll find that there is no better way.

Before I conclude, let me be more candid—stop fakin' it! While you are busy working at having counterfeit intimacy with women who you have no intentions of marrying, you are putting on a phony front to keep a certain image and posture. You're afraid that if a woman truly knew what she was dealing with, she would not stay committed to you. So you keep the relationship on a shallow level. What you don't realize is the value that this woman will bring to your life and that you need to make the decision to seriously commit to her.

God said that it is not good for man to be alone. This means the woman He created you for will support you in accomplishing what He has called you to do.

Since all men will not marry or are interested in marriage, God will be the support you need. He created for you a specific work and will make sure you achieve it when you seek Him. If it is your desire to marry, you ought to know that the woman (singular), not women (plural), whom God has for you is an essential part of you becoming the man that He has designed you to be. If you are not interested in getting married, you need to make sure not to toy with a woman's affections and have her think that the "friendship" with you will lead to marriage one day. Be open and honest and have integrity and tell her the truth. There are no valid excuses. Know that you have been designed and equipped to achieve your purpose. Hear from the Word of God the message that He has for you.

> **If it is your desire to marry, you ought to know that the woman (singular), not women (plural), whom God has for you is an essential part of you becoming the man that He has designed you to be.**

"For this is the will of God, your
sanctification; that is, that you abstain from
sexual immorality; that each of you know
how to possess his own vessel in sanctification
and honor, not in lustful passion, like the
Gentiles who do not know God; and that no
man transgress and defraud his brother in
the matter because the Lord is the avenger in
all these things, just as we also told you
before and solemnly warned you. For God has
not called us for the purpose of impurity, but
in sanctification. So, he who rejects this is not
rejecting man but the God who gives
His Holy Spirit to you."
—1 Thessalonians 4:3–8

Brothers, it is time to discover your identity and value in God. For you to be successful in your life, you have to find your peace and security in Him. Looking here, there, and everywhere is not going to get you anywhere. If you are serious about having a one-on-one, right relationship with God then you have to be honest with yourself, and give God your total being. He's the One who will work out the kinks that have been integrated into your life due to all of the "stuff" that has gone on in your life. He's the One who will cause you to "man up" in all that you do because of your decision to show your love for Him. He's the One who will lighten your load and minister to your heart. He's the

One who will take the undesirable desires away from you as you continue to turn toward Him and ask for His forgiveness. Once you discover that developing your character is paramount and begin to act like it, the rest will fall into place.

EVALUATE YOURSELVES, MY BROTHERS!

1. Where are you in the development of your masculinity?

2. If you have a sister or daughter, would you want her to be in a relationship or marry someone with a character similar to yours? If not, why?

3. If you grew up without a father or in a broken-home situation, do you want to allow the same pain that you experienced to harm your own family? Why or why not?

4. Are you portraying characteristics of honesty and integrity, commitment and responsibility, loyalty and devotion, humility and self-control? Why or why not? All of these traits exemplify true strength. Or are you a slave to your fleshly impulses for sex, money, and multiple sex partners? Why or why not?

5. Through the discovery process about yourself, what have you learned?

6. Have you had a life-changing encounter with your Creator? Why or why not?

7. Do you understand what God thinks about your lifestyle? Does your conscience agree with your behavior? Why or why not? Do you feel ashamed about the things that you do? Why or why not?

8. Do you feel ashamed about the things you do? Why or why not?

Brothers, it is time to discover your identity and value in God. For you to be successful in your life, you have to find your peace and security in Him.

These are some key questions to answer as you move toward experiencing the kind of life that God wants for you. God is a healer, and everybody needs to be healed in one way or another, if they're being honest with themselves. Ask Him to help you become stronger in the areas where you consciously know that you fall short. And in the areas where you may not recognize fault, ask Him to show you where you can make some changes and ask for the strength to make them. The process of being healed is the process of becoming more like God, who is Love, Life, and Goodness—everything that you need to make you whole. Is that something that you are interested in having in your life? Do you finally want to do things God's way? The Bible tells us that we all have fallen short of His glory. God's gift of Jesus giving His life for us is the example of what He would have us do for one another. Won't it make your life and the lives of others around you better, if you make the decision to follow Him? What's stopping you from wanting a right relationship with God? Do you feel like you can't let go of your past or what you are currently involved in? God's got the answer and will give you the wherewithal not only to love yourself, but to treat others with the love of Christ on a day-to-day basis. Give Him the chance to prove Himself to you. Man up!

Please read on. The next chapter will address how you can begin the process of becoming the man God created you to be.

7

In God We Trust

As I close, I trust that this book has been thought-provoking and enlightening. There are people out there who have decided to avoid seductive delusions by practicing abstinence until marriage, pursuing purity, and enjoying sex at its best.

I know that some readers may not agree with any of the points that I have made and will continue in whatever lifestyle they have already chosen. I'm not so naïve as to think that everyone will change their sexual behavior now that I have written a book. However, I also know that some may read what I have said, know in their hearts that it is right, but fear that their past wrongs have already disqualified them from living by the standard that I have advocated. These are the people that I want to address in this last chapter.

Continue to allow God to permeate your hearts and minds with the truth of His Word. He wants to begin the healing process with and for you today so that you can live a life of freedom from sin and shame.

> **I know that some readers may not agree with any of the points that I have made and will continue in whatever lifestyle they have already chosen.**

Sex at its best is sex the way that God intended it to be. I have based my stance on this subject on the authoritative word of the Bible. Scriptures related to my message are provided for you in Appendix B, "Doing It Right: Scriptural Aids to Walking in Victory," at the end of this book. I strongly suggest that you study them and meditate on them. As you spend time with Him, you will provide yourself with a priceless opportunity for God to speak to your heart concerning His Word.

I have alluded in each chapter to the idea that unhealthy behavior results from a lack of personal fulfillment. I want to say now that the only way to conquer personal emptiness and to fulfill your need for unconditional love is to have a relationship with God, your Creator. He made you and He knows what you need better than you do yourself.

There is a part of you that is spirit because you have been made in His image; it is made of the same "stuff" that God is made of. That is why I stress that only He can make you whole in your spirit. Because there is no match for His power, He can help you to relate to Him in a way that no one else can. When you have had a fresh encounter with God, it will be real and most effective—there will be no doubt in your mind that He has beckoned you to come to Him. I know for myself because it happened for me. Most of you know by now that I am a Christian, so I firmly believe that the only way to have a personal relationship with God is through Jesus—He died for that purpose.

If you have previously chosen a lifestyle that violates God's standards as He laid them out in the Bible, you can start over with a clean slate by receiving Jesus's gift of forgiveness and salvation. It's just that simple. Nothing complicated about it at all. That's the personal relationship that I'm talking about. I realize many of you were probably reared in a Christian home and you are familiar with Christian ideas. You may even be familiar with the "sinner's prayer" and can explain how and why you got saved. Having said this, if your knowledge about God doesn't cause you to pursue purity from a general standpoint, including sexual purity, then it's time to reexamine your salvation.

When you have had a fresh encounter with God, it will be real and most effective—there will be no doubt in your mind that He has beckoned you to come to Him.

For those of you who may have little or no background in the church, let me say this. The Bible records many claims that Jesus made about Himself. They include His claim that He was the Son of God; He is the only acceptable sacrifice that can make up for our sin. Jesus is the only Savior whom individuals can turn to in order to have their personal connection with God restored. Everyone who has heard of Jesus must decide for themselves about these claims: Was Jesus lying? Was He crazy? Or was He telling the truth?

If you believe that Jesus was telling the truth about Himself, take a moment to acknowledge your need for Him in your life. Express in your own words how it feels to be distant from Christ, and express your desire to know Him personally. Jesus will not only make Himself known to you, but He will give you a fresh start in all aspects of your life—including your sex life.

It's never too late to do this, no matter what kinds of things you have done or thought about doing, He is able to heal you, clean you up, and set you on track to live a life of purity. Furthermore, whether you have yet to be married or have a marriage that needs to be restored and made whole, Jesus is your Man. He is the One who knows how to make a marriage successful. He is the only One who has the power to change you. Do you believe that?

That's why we need the Bible; it shows us the way to change. All we need to do is follow God's instructions, and we will effect real change. It goes like this. When we openly confess that Jesus is Lord and believe in our hearts that God the Father raised Him from the dead, then we will be saved and restored to our place in Christ (see Romans 10:9–10). We will be freed from the chains of sin that have kept us from being who God created us to be. At that point we have become new creations in Christ—the old nature in us passes away and our new nature is born (see 2 Corinthians 5:17).

N o matter what kinds of things you have done or thought about doing, He is able to heal you, clean you up, and set you on track to live a life of purity.

After that, it is up to us to continue renewing our minds daily so that we won't forget that we have been given a new nature. It is this renewing of the mind that is so critical because it transforms us into the godly men and women that we are supposed to be (see Romans 12:2). Now we have the power within us to present our bodies as a sacrifice to God (see Romans 12:1). No longer are we slaves to lust, the lust that is sin.

Finally, remember that enjoying sex at its best is the opposite of dealing with seductive delusions. But the best kind of sex involves abstinence until marriage; The delusion of lust is not the way to go. So when temptation comes, be honest about it and talk to your Father in Heaven and ask Him to take those desires away from you. Continue to seek Him in and through those times, and rely on Him to bring you out of them. Kick, scream, and yell if you must, but after the tantrum give God the glory for His ever-present spirit that has rescued you, once again. No, it's not easy, but the character that you develop in the process of staying abstinent—along with a deepening relationship with God—is worth the sacrifice. Don't let anyone tell you that it is too late to begin practicing it. Because that simply isn't true. May you discover all that Jesus has for you and experience your life to the fullest.

> **May you discover all that Jesus has for you and experience your life to the fullest.**

Appendix A
Review Questions

1. What causes a spiritual transformation in one's life?
2. Where does the change take place when a person accepts Christ?
3. How does one recognize when an inward change has taken place?
4. What makes the change evident to others?
5. List three characteristics of love.
6. List three characteristics of lust.
7. How does behaving in lustful ways affect making good decisions about sex?
8. What is missing from the act of sex when it takes place outside of marriage?

9. What dominates a person's thoughts and actions before he or she accept Christ?

10. What is the most powerful motivating force for human behavior?

11. On what does one's self-worth depend?

12. In your opinion, would it take more determination to save sex for marriage than to yield to fleshly desires?

13. How does a couple demonstrate a commitment to love each other before marriage?

14. After making the decision to save sex for marriage, what is the best way to deal with sexual passion?

15. For singles, is it ever too late to become abstinent before marriage?

16. Why should sex be saved for marriage?

17. Why is sex emotionally safer within the context of marriage?

18. What makes the physical act of intercourse different emotionally and spiritually within marriage?

19. What two key things do you need to observe in a person with whom you are considering a serious relationship?

20. What has a person overlooked if they believe that they are not ready to commit their life to another person but at the same time they are

ready to give that person the most intimate part of themselves?

21. What are some of the possible reasons why marriages end in divorce for people who "live together" before marriage?

22. Why are condoms ineffective in protecting against sexually transmitted diseases?

23. Which virus is present in virtually all cases of cervical cancer?

24. What two important elements of human nature do the promoters of condoms omit from their awareness education?

25. What are the major differences between courtship and dating?

26. Use a concordance to search the Bible and find scriptures that address sexual purity.

27. What benefit do you receive when you consistently study and meditate on Scripture?

28. What is lost when someone believes their identity is based on how many people they have sex with? Why is this thinking delusional?

29. How will you make a difference in reversing the current cultural environment that has reduced sex to a casual act among consenting individuals?

30. What is a good working definition of pornography?

31. What massive industry plays a major role in distorting the realities about sex?

32. Name several misconceptions about sex than can be labeled as seductive delusions.

Appendix B
Doing It Right:
Scriptural Aids to Walking in Victory

Jesus said, *"If you love Me, you will keep My commandments"* (John 14:15). As believers in Christ Jesus, too often we are unaware of what we are commanded to do. We don't have an understanding of who we are released to be once Christ dwells within our hearts. So I wanted to provide some scriptural references for your personal reflection. As you study them, meditate on them, and apply them to your daily life, you will become empowered to stand against the temptations that surround us today.

I cannot emphasize this enough. In order for you to avoid the trap of seductive delusions, it takes more than just reading the Bible. It is imperative that you meditate on the Word of God so that it will always remind you of who you are in Christ.

Hear from the Word of God the benefits you will receive.

> *"How blessed is the man who does*
> *not walk in the counsel of the wicked,*
> *nor stand in the path of sinners,*
> *nor sit in the seat of scoffers!*
> *But his delight is in the law of*
> *the Lord, and in His law he*
> *meditates day and night.*
> *He will be like a tree firmly planted*
> *by streams of water, which yields*
> *its fruit in its season and its leaf*
> *does not wither; and in whatever*
> *he does, he prospers."*
> —Psalm 1:1–3

There are several insights we can draw from this passage:

1. When you do not surround yourself with people who are driven by delusions (the wicked, sinners, and mockers of God's Word), you allow yourself the freedom to enjoy the opposite of negative influence. Your desire and focus is to please the Lord. As a result,

the Word declares that you are blessed.

2. Instead of looking for gratification by being associated with ungodly people, you will find satisfaction and fulfillment in practicing God's way of life. You will have such a hunger for the Word of God that you will constantly dwell on it, think on it, roll it over in your mind as it relates to different areas of your life. You are giving the Word the opportunity to feed your heart with words of life and not death. That is what the process of meditation is all about.

3. Think about the image of a tree that is healthy and productive. It has great value and will flourish as long as it continues to receive nourishment. Now imagine yourself operating at the highest possible level of productivity in your life. The reality of this will only come about when you set your mind on pleasing God by obeying His commandments and following His will for your life. In turn, He will reward you with great blessings for the tremendous value that you bring to Him.

So I want to encourage you to feed upon the Scriptures below. They will nourish your heart with the divine nutrition that only comes from the power of God's Word. You will be properly prepared and equipped to live above seductive delusions!

THE VALUE OF SCRIPTURE

The following passages validate the power and vital significance of the Word of God. In order for us to gain the full benefit of God's Word, we must understand the extreme importance of applying it to our daily lives.

"For the word of God is living and active and sharper than any two-edged sword, and piercing as far as the division of soul and spirit, of both joints and marrow, and able to judge the thoughts and intentions of the heart."
—Hebrews 4:12

The Word of God penetrates through our intellect and emotions, exposing the very intentions of our heart. It has the ability to help us evaluate what is natural and spiritual and shows us the true motivation for our actions. We receive the greatest effectiveness of this process when we are transparent before God. It's in this place of openness that we see more clearly and transformation begins to take place.

"Be diligent to present yourself approved to God as a workman who does not need to be ashamed, accurately handling the word of truth."
—2 Timothy 2:15

The Word of God is the epitome of truth. For everyone who believes, it points the way to victory in life. In effect, God's Word is the light that we must follow in this dark world. We must never take the Word lightly because we are directed to make every possible effort to handle the truth with utmost respect and deference. Because we recognize the value of Scripture, we must not be passive readers but active students of the Word, seeking its deeper meanings and priceless truths.

> *"All Scripture is inspired by God and profitable for teaching, for reproof, for correction, for training in righteousness."*
> —2 Timothy 3:16

Some people try to justify rejecting certain passages of Scripture by positing that the Bible was a book written by mere men. That is only partially true because the writers of God's Word were divinely inspired by the Holy Spirit. God essentially used men as a means to channel His communication to us. No one has the right to pick and choose which parts of God's Word are acceptable and true, and in which are not. And there will be repercussions for attempting to do so.

For those who will simply try to alter God's Word and reduce Scripture to a form of literature that does not possess the power to transform lives, I simply have one question: Why would men write something that would ultimately condemn them to death? No one is excluded from the judgment that the Scripture professes, so it would be foolish to write about it if the impending judgment was untrue. Thankfully, there is a Savior who releases us from facing the verdict that men deserve when they do not obey Scripture and ultimately die in their sin.

CHRIST'S POWER WITHIN YOU

Many times we lose the battle to remain pure in all our ways because we forget who we are. If you have accepted Christ into your heart, then you have access to God's power and the ability to overcome every temptation known to man. I'm not saying that believers are perfect beings; however, for those who yield themselves to God consistently, you are in the process of being perfected in Christ.

"But as many as received Him, to them He gave the right to become children of God, even to those who believe in His name."
—John 1:12

Many people make the mistake of thinking they must be perfect prior to giving their hearts and minds over to God. In fact, this is actually a delusion. The only way to become like God is to put your faith and trust in God—just as you are. Notice in this Scripture that those who *receive* Him are the ones who *receive power* and the ability to *become* like Him. The closer that we associate ourselves with the Lord by believing in His name, the more we begin to imitate Him.

> *"You are from God, little children, and have*
> *overcome them; because greater is He who is*
> *in you than he who is in the world."*
> —1 John 4:4

This scripture warns us against following the teachings about Christ from anyone who presents themselves as a teacher of the Word of God but is actually a teacher of false doctrine. If a person is not led of the Holy Spirit, his interpretation of God's Word will not be accurate. He or she will deny the reality of the nature of Jesus Christ as God's Son who was both fully human and fully divine.

That is why it is so critical to personally study and meditate on God's Word. This way you will be able to determine if someone is giving you information about God that cannot be supported by His Word. You will overcome the influence of false teachers and refrain from being deceived by the one being referred to as "he who is in the world," known as the devil, the enemy of God.

If you have accepted Christ in your life, then He is real in your heart and no one can take that away from you. Unfortunately, it is possible to become distracted by various delusions and lose fellowship with Christ. Find a good church and fellowship with mature believers. Surround yourself with people who love God and are serious students of His Word. In this way you will stay in the Word and avoid allowing the world to appear "greater" than Christ in you. That is absolutely a delusion from which you must guard yourself!

"By this, love is perfected with us, so that we may have confidence in the day of judgment; because as He is, so also are we in this world."
—1 John 4:17

God is love and His love is in us. As we grow in Him, we grow in love (1 John 4:16). The more time we spend with Him, the more confidence we gain from our close association. Our thoughts and actions begin to reflect God's mind-set and His ways. We are the visible picture in this world of an invisible God.

"Seeing that His divine power has granted to us everything pertaining to life and godliness, through the true knowledge of Him who called us by His own glory and excellence."
—2 Peter 1:3

Notice that everything you need to live a life that is pleasing to God has been given to you through having the knowledge of who Christ is in all His glory. This is not intellectual knowledge; rather, it is the exchange of your heart's desire to live godly with Christ's power to sustain you in living for Him. The scripture points us toward vulnerability, tenderness, and stillness that come along with an intimate relationship with Christ. It is the same type of intimate bond that is established when a husband "knows" his wife in their wedding chamber. It is personal and exclusive.

One of the characteristics mentioned about Jesus is His glory, which is evident through His authority and power to bring us into fellowship with Him. The other is His excellence, which is also known as "virtue." We are to imitate Jesus's moral excellence in our behavior toward those around us. By being in an intimate relationship with Him and following His example, we are demonstrating an outward expression of a very real and personal bond with our Lord.

For instance, if there is a true bond between my wife and me, it will be evident to those around us. I have no right to give the appearance that I am single, because the reality is that I am married. In like manner, there should be external evidence that we have a bond with Christ that can be seen in the moral virtue demonstrated by our conduct.

THE RIGHT ATTITUDE

Many self-help materials and motivational speakers talk about the need to have a positive attitude. Having the right attitude is a biblical principle that is presented throughout Scripture and is reflected in proper Christian conduct.

> *"For as he thinks within himself, so he is."*
> —Proverbs 23:7

Your thoughts determine your actions and consequently develop into a pattern of behavior. Your behavior then dictates a certain lifestyle. Once you become a new creation in Christ, your desire should be to please God (2 Corinthians 5:17; Colossians 1:10). Even though you have been given a new nature, some changes must take place in your thought process. This is why it is so important to meditate and reflect on God's Word so that your mind can be continually renewed with the truth and your thought process will line up with who you are in Christ Jesus.

> *"Set your mind on the things above, not on the things that are on earth."*
> —Colossians 3:2

This scripture encourages us to direct our thoughts and desires toward God. Our priorities should be centered on following God's path to spending eternity with Him. Therefore, as believers, we must focus our attention on the things that are important to Him. It is tempting, however, to be distracted by the day-to-day events of this temporary existence. We must make a consistently decision to exercise self-discipline and not get caught up in the trivialities of life. Some people talk about being so "heavenly minded" that they are of "no earthly good." While that sounds like a legitimate concern, it really doesn't make sense. If you are truly heavenly minded, all you can be and do is earthly good.

> *"Therefore, since Christ has suffered in the flesh, arm yourselves also with the same purpose, because he who has suffered in the flesh has ceased from sin, so as to live the rest of the time in the flesh no longer for the lusts of men, but for the will of God."*
> —1 Peter 4:1–2

Notice that the instruction in this passage is to arm or protect yourself from your fleshly desires by following the same purpose that Christ followed. Clearly He made the decision and chose not to participate in sin. To respond to His will for us, we have a similar choice to make. We can choose to call that phone number and set up a rendezvous or delete it from our phones. We can choose to seek that person out over the Internet or cut off all forms of communication. We can choose to watch that movie, read that book, visit that website, or not. The choice to do the right thing at times is painful to our flesh, but the reward is much greater when we choose to do what God wants instead of what our flesh wants.

> *"Finally, brethren, whatever is true, whatever is honorable, whatever is right, whatever is pure, whatever is lovely, whatever is of good repute, if there is any excellence and if any-thing worthy of praise, dwell on these things."*
> —Philippians 4:8

We cannot always control what thoughts come to our mind, but we can choose which ones to embrace. This verse shares from the mind of God the kinds of things that we should allow our thoughts to settle on. From this list, a wonderful array of ideas should come to mind that will keep your thoughts pure and pleasing to God.

A CALL TO HOLINESS

Are you a parent? Have you had the opportunity to raise children and watch over their growth? Whether you are or not, to some degree you know a little something about the bond between a parent and child. Probably, you shared your childhood with a parent, guardian, or some other person who was responsible for your development.

Children need to be taught right from wrong. Those who take the teaching role seriously understand that nurturing children means striving to invest in them every bit of constructive training and guidance possible. It stands to reason that the more one invests in a child, the more positive results the parental figure will observe in that child's thinking and behavior. Through proper discipline, parents set expectations and children learn that their best behavior is not an optional action—it is the right and acceptable choice to make.

In a similar way, we have to understand that holiness is not optional in our relationship with Christ. In actuality, living a godly life is fulfilling the call to reflect the image and likeness of who He is. Furthermore, it would be impossible to commune with Christ on a daily basis and not become more like Him. But at the same time, we must understand that the transformation doesn't happen overnight—it is a lifelong process.

As a matter of fact, even the hard things that we go through in life are designed to provide us with the proper discipline that helps us grow in Christ. As believers, we need to be molded into followers of Christ so that, as the writer of Hebrews defines the process, *"we may share His holiness"* (Hebrews 12:10; italics added). The good news is that Jesus does not leave us to our own devices in the pursuit of holiness. Believers share a covenant with Him where He provides us with forgiveness, redemption, justification, protection, deliverance, and salvation. I might add that we would not have access to any of these life-changing blessings if it were not for Jesus.

On the other hand, if you say that you belong to Him, but you choose a lifestyle that does not reflect who you are in Him, then you are simply practicing religious routines. This type of behavior will prevent you from enjoying the full experience of being a child of God. The apostle Paul understood the distinction between the choice to live a holy life that is pleasing to God and the choice to live a life of self-gratification. Listen to his pressing appeal.

"Therefore I urge you, brethren, by the mercies of God, to present your bodies a living and holy sacrifice, acceptable to God, which is your spiritual service of worship."
Romans 12:1

Paul wanted those who claim to know Christ to know that there is a lifelong commitment involved. We need to recognize the responsibility we have toward God, realizing that we did not create ourselves. As a result, the very least we can do is fully submit to the One who did. Not with mere lip service or fake sincerity, but with one's entire being—heart, soul, and body—must we live in holy submission to His will.

God created us to worship and serve Him. But we can only do that when we obey His instructions. Of course, He has also given us free will, and we have the freedom to willingly choose Him or not. But once you receive Christ into your heart by faith, you begin to realize all that He has done for you. Since He has given you the chance to live a truly satisfying life here on earth and the ultimate reward of spending eternity with Him, your natural response should be to give yourself fully over to His service. The Bible says that it is the most reasonable response you can offer Him. And guess what? You won't be disappointed that you did.

There is no greater feeling than to know that you are on the right side of life and you're trying your best to live a life that honors God. But it's all about doing it His way. When you realize this and make it a part of your day-to-day living, you will sense within yourself that all is well with your soul. Remember that the Word of God says to submit your body to God. It will be a sacrifice worth making, and it's all wrapped up in a little thing called obedience. When you obey God's commands, you won't find yourself trapped by the seductive delusions lurking about, waiting to entangle anyone who will fall for them. Instead, the result of obedient behavior toward God is found in His directive to us:

Seductive Delusions

"As obedient children, do not be conformed to the former lusts which were yours in your ignorance, but like the Holy One who called you, be holy yourselves also in all your behavior; because it is written, 'YOU SHALL BE HOLY, FOR I AM HOLY.'"
—1 Peter 1:14–16

From the very beginning of time, God declared Himself holy. He is the embodiment of holiness (see Leviticus 20:7). Now Scripture is calling us to make the decision to be holy out of obedience to God, our heavenly Father. The first step is receiving Christ and His gift of salvation. After we receive the new nature that comes along with salvation in Christ, we are cautioned to find the path of holiness. Christ set us apart from our sinful ways and He desires for us to dedicate ourselves to a life that glorifies Him. It is a continuous process, where we must make the decision to change the behavioral pattern of our former lives as nonbelievers. By choosing to live holy on a daily basis, we will not easily revert to the "former lusts" that we were once driven by.

Following the counsel of God's Word will always lead us in the right direction—toward God and not away from Him. Here is some insight into how to go about ensuring that you won't miss the greatest opportunity of and the reason for your very existence:

"Pursue peace with all men, and
the sanctification without which
no one will see the Lord."
—Hebrews 12:14

This verse reveals some critical elements that we need in preparation for being with the Lord. We are to practice living in peace with others. You'll know you're on the right track when you don't allow people to rattle you and "push buttons" that would have previously set you off on a tirade. Scripture offers the welcome promise of peace by confessing to God:

"Those who love Your law have
great peace, and nothing
causes them to stumble."
—Psalm 119:165

You may be wondering what "law" the Scripture is referring to—the thing that Scripture says we must love in order to acquire the peace of God. Well, wonder no more. Someone once asked Jesus the question,

"'Teacher, which is the great
commandment in the Law?'"
—Matthew 22:36

And Jesus answered,

*"'"YOU SHALL LOVE THE LORD YOUR GOD
WITH ALL YOUR HEART, AND WITH ALL
YOUR SOUL, AND WITH ALL YOUR MIND."*
This is the great and foremost commandment.'"
—Matthew 22:37–38

Being the most excellent Teacher that ever lived, He didn't stop there. In describing what it takes to obey God's commandments, Jesus followed up the first and greatest commandment with the second one:

"'"YOU SHALL LOVE YOUR NEIGHBOR
AS YOURSELF."
On these two commandments depend
the whole Law and the Prophets.'"
—Matthew 22:39–40

My point is that there is no way that you can leave out practicing love God's way and consider yourself a holy and righteous human being. So make sure that you love God first and put Him above everything else in your life. Follow that up with loving everyone else whom you encounter. And finally, don't forget the most crucial element of peaceful living: love yourself. You will find that there won't be a whole lot that people and situations can do to trip you up. It's the way to find true peace.

Moreover, consecrate yourself to the Lord by answering the call to holiness and sanctification. That means, put a lot of distance between you and your old ways and habits. People who are familiar with you should notice a distinct difference in your attitude and actions. But thankfully, we do not have to do this on our own. Jesus shed His blood and died on the cross for us so that we could be holy. Our job is to believe in the work that He did and receive it as a gift called salvation.

He made the way possible. You see, Jesus rescued us and covered us under His blood, freeing us from a life of sin. The Word of God explains: *"But now in Christ Jesus you who formerly were far off have been brought near by the blood of Christ"* (Ephesians 2:13). So determine within yourself that you will do whatever it takes to closely associate yourself with Him. Don't worry; when He sees the sincerity of your heart, you will experience the power that you need to make this a reality for you.

In fact, there is unimaginable power in the blood of Jesus. Scripture tells us that it is the blood of Jesus that cleanses us from all sin (see 1 John 1:7). As long as we acknowledge Him and show that we love Him by obeying the commandments that He gave us, we're all good. We can join with the apostle Paul who said,

"For I am not ashamed of the gospel of Christ: for it is the power of God unto salvation to every one that believeth."
—Romans 1:16 KJV

Through Christ, we have been given everything that pertains to godliness. But at the end of the day, it comes down to how much we commit to living a life of holiness and purity. As a final exhortation, listen to the wise words of Scripture that show us the way to dedicate ourselves to Christ and to live a virtuous life:

"Therefore, having these promises, beloved, let us cleanse ourselves from all defilement of flesh and spirit, perfecting holiness in the fear of God."
—2 Corinthians 7:1

We have been given access to God through the work that Christ did on our behalf. Now it's up to us to confess our sins when we miss the mark and commit sin. This is not the time to run away from God; rather, we need to run to Him with a repentant heart. Let's be honest. There are times when we fall prey to sin. It may be by giving more attention to acquiring things than to making God our first priority. It may be putting more focus on a relationship with someone than on pursuing God. It may be having bitterness and an unforgiving heart toward someone who caused us deep hurt. Maybe it's choosing to watch a TV show when we know that we should be renewing our minds by studying Scripture, meditating on the Word, and praying.

Whatever it may be, please hear me: Know that becoming perfected in Christ is a continual process.

So don't be afraid to admit to God when you fall short. This is what He wants, an open channel of communication with you so that you can enjoy heart-to-heart communion with Him. It shows God the utmost respect and honor. So, with the power God has given you, cleanse yourself from impure conduct and ill feelings that only keep you stuck in the past. Once you get some perspective on how much God loves you and wants to be your first intimate relationship, before all others, you will be truly amazed by the way that God will make Himself real to you.

Acknowledgments

Many thanks to September 9 Media & Management. Terhea Washington and her staff helped me to plant the seed and they are standing with me as we watch the Lord bring in a harvest of souls who are committed to living in sexual purity.

To my family: my grandmother NanaHenry, who is responsible for a lot of my leadership strength, and my grandmother Nana Day, who from the time I was a very young man, imparted a deep yearning in my heart to know God. I love you and I am thankful for you both.

To my in-laws in Louisiana, Donald and Jacqueline Barquet, whose Southern love and sweetness cannot be compared to anything else on earth.

To my parents, Lawrence and Carol Henry, who always gave me the best of everything they had, and instilled in me the belief that I could achieve whatever I dreamed. I pray that I will always bring honor to your name.

To my lovely wife, Terry, you are truly God's treasure from heaven in my life. I am grateful for your love, support, and sacrifice. Thank you for allowing me to share with the world what God has imparted to me.

—GERARD W. HENRY

Notes

1. "Don't Believe the Hype!" Generation Life website http://www.generationlife.org/life_love/stds.php. Also: "Adolescents at Risk: Statistics on HIV/AIDS, STDs and Unintended Pregnancy. Illinois Department of Public Health, http://www.idph.state.il.us/public/respect/hiv_fs.htm.

2. "Use of Contraceptives and Use of Family Planning Services in the United States" report, p. 11. *Advance Data from Vital and Health Statistics*, CDC No. 350, December 10, 2004.

3. "Condoms and STDs: Fact Sheet for Public Health Personnel." Center for Disease Control (CDC) website, http://www.cdc.gov/condomeffectiveness/brief.html.

4. "Condom Use by Adolescents." American Academy of Pediatrics. AAP Policy website, http://aappolicy.aappublications.org/cgi/content/full/pediatrics;107/6/1463.

5. "Condoms and STDs: Fact Sheet for Public Health Personnel."

6. "The CDC Fact Sheet on Chlamydia." Centers for Disease Control and Prevention website, http://www.cdc.gov/STD/chlamydia/STDFact-Chlamydia.htm.

7. "The CDC Fact Sheet on Genital Herpes." Centers for Disease Control and Prevention website, http://www.cdc.gov/STD/Herpes/STDFact-Herpes.htm.

8. "IWF Alert on Condom Warning Labels." Independent Women's Forum website, http://iwf.org/iwfmedia/show/18356.html.

9. Robert T. Michael, John H. Gagnon, Edward O. Laumann, and Gina Kolata. *Sex in America: A Definitive Survey.* Boston: Little, Brown & Company (published by arrangement with Warner Books, New York) 1995) p. 124.

10. "Debunking Divorce Myths," David Popenoe. Discovery Health website, http://health.discovery.com/centers/loverelationships/ articles/divorce.html.

11. Dr. Don Raunikar, a professional therapist, specialized in dealing with the issues of singles until his death in 2004. After many years of addressing the day-to-day hopes and concerns of his patients, he wrote *Choosing God's Best: Wisdom for Lifelong Romance* (Multnomah, 2006) to promote healthy relationships.

HOOKED

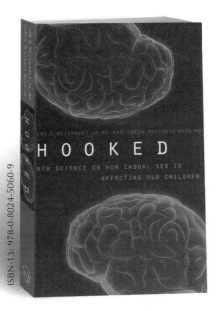

ISBN-13: 978-0-8024-5060-9

Society tells us that sex is an act of self-expression, a personal choice for physical pleasure that can be summed up in the ubiquitous phrase "hooking up." Millions of American teenagers and young adults are finding that the psychological baggage of such behavior is having a real and lasting impact on their lives. They are discovering that "hooking up" is the easy part, but "unhooking" from the bonds of a sexual relationship can have serious consequences.

A practical look into new scientific research showing how sexual activity causes the release of brain chemicals which then results in emotional bonding and a powerful desire to repeat the activity. This book will help parents and singles understand that "safe sex" isn't safe at all; that even if they are protected against STDs and pregnancy, they are still hurting themselves and their partner.

MOODY
PUBLISHERS
moodypublishers.com

LIFT EVERY VOICE BOOKS

Lift every voice and sing
Till earth and heaven ring,
Ring with the harmonies of Liberty;
Let our rejoicing rise
High as the listening skies,
Let it resound loud as the rolling sea.
Sing a song full of the faith that the dark past has taught us,
Sing a song full of the hope that the present has brought us,
Facing the rising sun of our new day begun
Let us march on till victory is won.

The Black National Anthem, written by James Weldon Johnson in 1900, captures the essence of Lift Every Voice Books. Lift Every Voice Books is an imprint of Moody Publishers that celebrates a rich culture and great heritage of faith, based on the foundation of eternal truth—God's Word. We endeavor to restore the fabric of the African-American soul and reclaim the indomitable spirit that kept our forefathers true to God in spite of insurmountable odds.

We are Lift Every Voice Books—Christ-centered books and resources for restoring the African-American soul.

For more information on other books and products
written and produced from a biblical perspective, go to
www.lifteveryvoicebooks.com or write to:

Lift Every Voice Books
820 N. LaSalle Boulevard
Chicago, IL 60610
www.lifteveryvoicebooks.com